S0-CFB-159

OWLS HEAD

O W L S   H E A D

Rosamond Purcell

THE QUANTUCK LANE PRESS

Copyright © 2003 by Rosamond Purcell
All rights reserved
Printed in the United States and Italy
First Edition
Design by Laura Lindgren
The text of this book is set in Wessex
with display type in Poliphilus Titling.
Manufactured by Maple-Vail

Library of Congress Cataloging-in-Publication Data
Purcell, Rosamond Wolff.

Owls Head / Rosamond Purcell.

p.   cm.

ISBN 0-9714548-6-8

1. Purcell, Rosamond Wolff—Friends and associates.
2. Buckminster, William, 1922– Anecdotes. 3. Antique
dealers—Maine—Owls Head—Anecdotes. 4. Women
photographers—United States—Anecdotes.
5. Photographers—United States—Anecdotes. I. Title.
TR140.P87P87 2003
770'.92—dc21   2003008538

The Quantuck Lane Press
Distributed by
W. W. Norton & Company, Inc.
500 Fifth Avenue, New York, NY 10110
W. W. Norton & Company Ltd.
Castle House, 75/76 Wells Street, London W1T 3QT

1 2 3 4 5 6 7 8 9 0

To Dennis

Who is there?

The reader is there—

talking back

I

BREAKING GROUND

"*Don, lo cauecs vos ahura,*
Que tals bad'en la peintura Qu'atre n'espera la mana."
[Sir, the owl warns you:
this one gapes at the painting, another waits for manna.]
—Marcabru, *L'autrier jost' una sebissa*
(troubadour pastorela, twelfth century)

THE CURATOR'S NOTE below the open termite-eaten book at the Museum of Comparative Zoology read: *Found in the basement of Harvard Hall during renovations.* The foraging by the insects had been most thorough. The pages looked like a stack of thin sandwiches after children had dug into the soft parts—eaten the butter, the meat, and most of the bread—but left untouched, as despised, the delicate crusts. Printed in French in eighteenth-century type, the lumps of uneaten matter stood high like islands on a relief map. Piles of sandy-orange termite leavings were packed into the crevices throughout. I had never seen anything like it.

When the exhibition closed, I asked to photograph this cultural skeleton. The termites had consumed most of the text down to the back of the book and deep into the spine. They had chosen, too, what not to eat, rejecting the words *Moscou . . . des villes anciennes*, avoiding *Si son père* and also *fils*. These and a few perhaps less delectable jigsaw pieces constituted the entire remains of the original text. Later I learned that termites prefer their paper damp, a damp that dissipated near the outer edges, which explained why the borders of the pages had been preserved and why, when the book was closed, there was no outward sign of destruction.[1]

I, too, have eaten paper from old books. I remember as a girl tearing and eating the corners of pages as I read. Victorian paper tastes dry—better, actually, than the paper used in newer books, which, if uncoated, tastes dull like chalk, or, if glossy, like tilefish or squid. When I ate the paper I took each corner the way one takes a communion wafer, flat on the tongue, feeling it dissolve. I ate not from hunger but because the page came to hand. I ate my way especially through the corners of the *Elsie Dinsmore* books. [2] My mother (who used to eat library paste and paper too) said that both of us must have suffered from a dietary deficiency. Therefore I am free to blame my behavior on an inherited craving.

Growing up, I read many books from my parents' and grandparents' libraries, and extended my literary foraging into nineteenth-century stories that had little to do with my own. Whenever my father, a professor of Byzantine history and Victorian literature, came across one of his four children wandering about in what he perceived to be an aimless fashion, he would ask, "Where's your book?" When I showed the photograph I'd made of the termite-eaten book to my father, he said nothing about the entomological flourishes. He considered the islands. He read across the chasms to conclude that in the mid-nineteenth century, in order to seek their fortunes, younger men from Russian farms began to migrate to the cities—hence, "Si le père…un metier…Villes…compagnes…Moscou." Therefore the economic balance, he explained, shifting from the country to the city, eventually began to work against the farmers. As always, my father extracted the most meaning from the least available text. Why had I not read for content by jumping from island to island? Charmed by the *lack* of text, I reveled in *not* having to read this book, as well as in the freedom of adding my own footnotes. Before photographing it I had stuffed the cavities with butterfly wings to extend the metaphor of regeneration implicit in *père et fils*, father and son.[3] That, in a way, is my profession now, to take a hint from something small and build on what I see. I learned so much from this gnawed book. But it was the second one that sealed my fate.

For a week in the summer of 1981 I taught a course called "Developing Your Personal Vision" at the Photographic Workshops, the East Coast mecca for photographers in Rockport, Maine. A diffidence toward the classroom and most public events extends into middle age as I resist attending academic lectures, openings, and galleries—in short, in tuning in to the very frequencies I supposedly operate on. I don't like teaching much either but, because I do like students, I was honored to be in Rockport. I will, in time, forget the classroom, but not what we found along the way.

For the first hours, in the darkened studio with the slide projector, I stuck to the catalogue description of the class. One student was recovering from her life to date and hoped photography would save her; another was making a book out of mediocre work; a third, complaining that the class was not as advertised, left to join another; while two older women from Kansas City on a mission from the Hallmark card company projected slides of sunsets and sailboats on the wall. These last two seemed to suffer from less personal malaise than the rest—adrift, as I feared we already were, in an unphotographable miasma of self-examination. The Hallmark women had come to scope out a particular photographic technique I had developed—that of combining nineteenth-century glass ambrotypes with printed drawings of animals. Closely layered translucent plates created ambiguous crossover beings I then recorded on film. I brought out pictures of a half man–half owl, a bear-snouted woman with ringlets, and a boy cradling his human elbow in his gorilla hand.

As a photographer, I have a tendency to see things doubled—like an anableps with two sets of eyes, one above and one below the water. I want the surface and also whatever lies beneath. There is a satisfying density in the vision of a grandmother merging into an orangutan and a spinster with tadpole legs growing—*proud flesh*—from her cheeks. These Dr. Moreau–like apparitions broke the curse of the predictable in what was then a pre-Photoshop world. Victorians—as in *Elsie Dinsmore*—are often irritating. I wanted to shake the people in these ambrotypes out of their brooches, breeches, and sateen dresses and send them naked and hairy back into the trees. To achieve this interspecial effect, I'd remove the ambrotype midway through the exposure leaving the printed beast to bleed through human joints. It took a lot of animal to dissolve the heavy clothes. I demonstrated the technique to the class. The arcane process—once so exciting to me—was irrelevant to these students. Not everyone wants to turn people into animals. Most, although I provided suggestive props, didn't even want to try. The Hallmark pair, however, were eager to hit the antiques shops for glass plates of pretty women, pressed flowers, and lace. We decided to go outside.

That day went on forever. In a meandering caravan of cars, we visited an old graveyard where I held forth on the beauty of historical patinas lent by lichen and acid rain, until someone said, "There's nothing here to photograph." Chastened, we moved on. An hour later, on the road to the Owls Head lighthouse, we came across a colorful pile of lobster buoys, several weathered buildings, and then, high behind the old-growth trees, we saw it: jagged hills of scrap metal looming like glinting crests of water or like dismantled dinosaur parts. In heaps and mounds and prodigious hills the junk surged above us. We took our cameras, tripods, and water bottles and walked into the hills. The ground was covered with lobster traps, household pots and pans, piles and stacks of wooden shutters. It was the most covered ground I'd ever seen. On the periphery of the mountains, a small unsmiling person appeared and said—not much. His name was William Buckminster and he must have said it was okay to walk around, to take pictures, and to buy whatever we found outside or from a house marked ANTIQUES, because we did. I don't remember much photography from that day; the sun was hot and most of us drunk on the novelty of rural eccentricity and unfathomable chaos. The steep mounds were tight-packed and tumbling; I could feel the pressure of even more hidden under the slopes and the foundations of the buildings.

While the students stepped out to explore the acres of battered antique household and industrial objects, I hesitated. A few made for the shop and eventually emerged carrying loads of sheet music, chandeliers, and horseshoes. Others scaled the slopes with a fine bang-crashing of metal against metal and disappeared from view. Later we learned that one had spent the hours beating the bounds of the property like a human tape measure, down to the sloping rim of the backyard and beyond, up the dirt road—eleven acres in all, and all of it loaded with stuff. Climbing a mound the others reached the top and said, "*Wow*." All they would say after that was that there was much more *out there*. In the throes of discovery, they had no time to talk. I tried to climb the scrap-metal hills, dislodged the battered top layer, slipped on the tumbling scree, and slid back down. The straps of my sandals caught on wires from lamps, car radiators, and broken radios. Physically hesitant at the best of times, I needed boots, perhaps crampons.

To haul myself over the small pipes and plumbing washers that rolled in a stream under my feet, I grabbed crisscross braces of scaffolding. The wood wobbled and swayed so I went back to slipping on my own down a crooked course covered with coiling, curving objects and through a mirrored canyon of plumbing pipes and joints, whose surfaces reflected the sky. I could not tell what many objects were or even what they were made of. A grey cloth draping a lawn mower was heavy as lead; I stubbed my foot against an old newspaper that turned out to be a lump of cement. When I lifted a metal box, one end collapsed into red dust in my hands. Here was a truck tire full of rainwater floating pretty dishes, there what seemed to be organ pipes, a miniature bed of nails, an iron lung, and a corpselike rubber baby doll leaking foam. While admiring an unbroken porcelain bowl that lay under a piano stool and a brass chandelier I hit my shoulder on a brace of andirons, almost toppling this improbable tower. How could it be that under such pressure the bowl had not lost a chip? Beside me rose a mountain—twenty feet high at least and who knew how wide, composed almost entirely of aluminum furniture and crumpled pots. There were no paths. It was overwhelming.

I stumbled back to the antiques shop. The building was well braced by the pipe canyon on one side and a pile of electrical castoffs on the other. Wire baskets of bottles on the porch glinted like scarecrow flashers. Even the tunneled path (an obvious concession by the owner) held its pitfalls: a pan of rusted water tipped over onto my feet; hidden wires, some only as thick as grass, attacked from all sides. The door, when I reached it, opened just wide enough for a person to squeeze in sideways. Ahead in the dim interior, four or five of my group slowly labored, as if roped together on a perilous expedition, across the object-strewn floor. It smelled moldy, "like a mausoleum," someone said, stumbling past in retreat. A quick glimpse at the ceiling revealed a tangle of wire hangers, a broken neck halter for a horse, and faded paper Christmas bells. I focused on a lamp base with vestiges of violet silk like the skirt from a doll—*It is the same doll*, I thought, repelled. At a certain age I was presented with a sequence of "bridesmaid dolls," a pre-Barbie dressed in various outfits. I loved to receive these dolls; I especially loved the sight of the white with blue or pink polka-dot box they came strapped in. But even though I asked for and received whichever one I didn't yet have—the Señorita doll, the Marie Antoinette doll—I was always disappointed. No matter what the ethnic or historical trappings, underneath it was the same doll. Here now was the skirt from the Southern Belle, filthy and disreputable; I would know it anywhere, like all those things we throw away but never can be rid of.

I did not follow the hard-core shoppers into the choking air of the second room. I heard the footsteps of someone above my head—oh no, a second floor.

Outside it was fresh, geological, safer. Under the tough pines close to the piles of buoys were stacks of six-paned window frames wedged sill-deep into the ground and surrounded by shattered glass. Chairs, tables, sewing machines, bell buoys, and the pieces of a tugboat filled in the bare spots. There was an inside-out quality to the landscape. These domestic and maritime fittings now belonged to the earth. Nearby were perhaps fifty wooden lobster traps neatly stacked, moss forming on top of barnacles that covered the wooden slats and petaled lichen on the clipped grey ropes—sign of a longtime mingling of land and sea.

This dumping ground seemed to be a private enterprise, for one of the houses on the end boasted a rag-filled laundry line and oil drums stacked up against the walls as if for winter fuel. Two worn cars stood beside this house with roofs so camouflaged by objects it was as though they formed the base for new mountains. As the cars themselves were not yet buried, I could see the interiors bulging with shovels, trunks, old tools, and oars. Creased painted sheets of copper, many feet across and pierced as if by bullets, loomed over the cars. Beyond these I made out a sign, DANGER OF ELECTROCUTION, set in front of a hill of tangled chandeliers, lamps, and a wormy mass of plastic-covered electrical cords stacked to overflowing in bushel baskets. Electrical wires dipped low from the eaves of the shop. I could hear the fleeting voices of my companions, seagulls, and the sound of someone chopping.

In rural New England poverty and thrift go hand in hand: waste not, want not. It is good country wisdom to keep old stoves, extra windows, and car parts. You never know what you will need, or when. But here was an exaggeration of all the other Down East front yards we'd passed along the way. It was mysterious in its excess. It was as if a magnet had dragged several hotels, a waterfront, and a whole town up or down the coast to this spot. And yet what seemed born of a grand unearthly gesture or a series of maelstroms was actually an all-American trash heap. This yard surely held a virtual museum of the cultural detritus of Maine, compressed onto a few acres. And, as museum collections often are, it was both overstocked and shabby.

The Hallmark women emerged from the antiques shop with a box of perfect lace and ancient valentines. Someone else with a stack of records—Big Band! Boy, was I a lousy shopper. What had I missed?

One of the students joined me by the lobster pots and we began to inspect the front yard. Stumbling over the uneven terrain we came upon the kind of canvas used to cover a fresh-dug grave. Underneath, moldering away, were dozens of books dating from the 1940s and '50s. We dug down deeper through the mound until, reaching the ground and finding books sunk even deeper, we lay down in the tall grass and hauled them out using our arms as shovels. For the rest of the afternoon we excavated the subterranean library, moving away from time to time to make tentative forays into the rest of the yard, but drawn always back to the book hole. Mesmerized, we studied the impressive range of decay that New England seasons bestow on cloth and paper. Admiring the stained-glass colors of the streaked covers, the partial, enigmatic paragraphs, and the thickened claylike tablets of once ordinary books, we lugged the stacks from the shaft to the owner of the place and with sincere desire asked to buy them. Almost as sincerely, he sold them to us. Nowhere to be seen throughout our visit, Mr. Buckminster materialized as the afternoon waned and the rest of the group came forward with their own dubious loads. Nature, too, was up for sale it seemed, as Buckminster charged something for everything, a dollar for a gnarled tree limb and two for a beach stone ringed with a white band. He transcribed each purchase into a small notebook, using carbon paper, consulting price tags (when there were price tags), and entering the name of the object followed by a letter-number code: VALENTINE, T654, $1.00. His fingernails were like shaly yellow shells. As he asked almost nothing for the books, I offered to pay a little more. He looked at me like I was nuts. "But this is the kind of thing I'd take to the dump," he said. "What will you do with them?" I told him the books were worth a lot to us, although I couldn't explain why. He shrugged and kept on figuring. We carried away carton after carton of terminal rot.

At the time, I was both fascinated and shocked by the condition of the disinterred books. They confirmed a collusion between willful neglect and the indifference of nature. I wanted to acquire the lot because it was full of visual incident. As I am descended from generations of collectors on both sides of the family, perhaps by genetic default I was in the throes that day of becoming a collector myself.

I began to feel indistinct longings for things I'd never seen before. I found it touching that these sodden bug-webbed books had not fallen apart. Nor had they vanished—even when placed underground. Destined to vanish, they had not. "Fetishism is a co-mingling of affection and revulsion," wrote a learned friend some years later of my fascination with this condition.[4]

And while I struggle step by step and in nonacademic language to define what the concept of *fetishism* means to me as a person who repeatedly falls in love (for it feels like love to me) with *the way things look*, it will take the length of this book to explain the ways in which this love manifests itself.

The next day, my fellow excavator entered the dark classroom and held out a bundle. "For you," she said. Two volumes, stuck together horizontally, had been converted into some kind of nest. The pages on one end remained more or less intact; at the other end lay the compact straw and paper nest, made, we decided, by a mouse. Interwoven in the straw were syllables and occasional words. By peeling back the fragments to a certain depth, we could read the title of the upper story of the nest as

Flying Hostesses of the Air. To read the title of the second book we would have had to destroy it.

Here was a variation on the termite-eaten book, another example of how nonhumans undermine texts printed by humans, the mice, this time, making light weight of light reading. Not since the termite-eaten book had I witnessed such virtuosity in the destruction of text inside or outside a museum showcase. I recognize the gnawings of beavers, dogs, bore holes in all kinds of wood and the nests of paper wasps and birds, but I had never seen such an elegant display of animal infiltration into the realm of pulp fiction. My coworker had found the book-nest by digging laterally into the pit. Near the surface, under the rock ledge and protected by an upper layer of weather-bearing books, the underpinnings of *Hostesses*, flaky as baklava, fell into her hands. In retrospect, I was ready for this seminal object or, as the historian Krzysztof Pomian describes such allusion-laden manifestations, this *semaphore*, to push me over the edge into full-blown collecting.[5]

That evening I drove back to Owls Head and, in the mellow light, poked again inside the trench. I plowed through the moldy layers we'd left behind, down to the last volumes laid end to end on a board. Long sunk under the weight of the books, the wood was now rotten, entangled with roots and earth. From the blend of text and soil I felt that something inexplicably cogent was beginning to grow.

In the twenty years since that summer I have made dozens of visits to Buckminster's property and taken thousands of objects home. Like the archaeologist or Egyptologist that, as a fifth grader, I decided I would become, I kept digging. And like an archaeologist I have become territorial about this—my—place. When the book pit was empty, I moved on, wanting to see *everything* and so always bring new fortune home.

Now, two decades later, the book-nest is in my studio in a glass-front cabinet, under a Plexiglas lid. Once every five years or so I make a list of the random letters and disconnected syllables that continue to drop from the straw. And the hunger that its appearance awakened in me does not go away.

2

INFILTRATION

I placed a jar in Tennessee.
And round it was, upon a hill.
It made the slovenly wilderness
Surround that hill.

—"Anecdote of the Jar,"
Wallace Stevens

"I THOUGHT IT WAS going to be fields of old cars," said a friend as we drove into Buckminster's front yard. I didn't know he lived here, too." "You never said it was a *compound*," complained another several years later; "or that he owned all those buildings." Of course I had—at least, I thought I had—they just weren't listening. Even after many visits spent gaping and gathering, it appeared I had failed to describe the vastness, disorder, and gentle melancholy of the place. Nothing I say before we arrive impresses my friends. "You'll love it," I'd insist, to talk them into coming along. "It's better than all the other places."

Located on a point of land near Rockland, Maine, the center of Owls Head[1] consists of a flagpole, a triangular garden bed, a miniature post office, and a two-room general store. Across the street are two almost conjoined ponds, where, in the spring and summer, cattails, frogs, fish, cormorants, red-wing blackbirds, and yellow iris flourish, and in the winter, icy mounds of aquatic grass crack and refreeze. The pond nearest the road is grey-blue and lovely, the second thick with rushes and reeds.

The fire department siphons water from the ponds and boys attempt to fish, although most of the fish (goldfish deposited from a nearby summer camp years ago, grown into full-sized carp) are scooped up by the osprey and cormorants. Sometimes a kingfisher perches on the electrical wires and dives for the carp that once were gold and now (in response to their environment) are as dim as mud. The back pond, created by a dam Buckminster built, belongs to him, as do the woods on either side of a dirt road leading to one of the two town cemeteries. The woods are old, composed of spruce and poplar, maple, oak, fir, and a single fifty-foot-high hemlock. Crows perch on the top of this tree above the spare and sandy ground. On a ridge above, about twenty feet from the pond, Buckminster lives in a hundred-and-fifty-year-old house that was originally the town's first post office. I had surmised—I was wrong—that he lived on land and in a house inherited from his wife Helen Wormwood's family. He also owns a barn, a cottage by the water, a family house once lived in by a sea captain and his heirs, and a fourth house, originally a stable, next a dry goods and penny candy shop, and most recently the antiques shop. Except for the swamp-level guest house built in the 1920s, the buildings above the dirt road that leads to the cemetery date from various decades of the nineteenth century.

By the fifties Buckminster chose to trade in scrap metal and with Helen ran the antiques business that deteriorated after she died. Now all but the shop and his house are sealed and posted with threatening signs. Buckminster seemed a gentle man, but as the entryway to his house featured a photocopy of a snarling German shepherd, for all I knew he had a taste for violence and reprisal. If I barged too far into his world, would he unchain some rampaging beast?

Buckminster was also a reticent man and I had been brought up to believe that one didn't *do* certain things: *Personal remarks avoid and no one will be annoyed*, my mother used to say, quoting her grandmother. I knew that scrap-metal dealers specialized in pulling things apart and that this waste was a natural outcome of the business of obsolescence, wreckage, and scavenging, but this particular chaos seemed personal, beyond business. I didn't know how it had happened or what questions to ask.

But then I'd come across barred doors to the houses full of things. I'd excavate merchandise Buckminster would refuse to sell and I would wonder why. I came across a spiral staircase in the woods, a bicycle embedded up to the handle bars in the base of a hill, a child's coffin, and in a nearby tree, precisely hung, a fisherman's lantern. I came across a secret room in the back of a truck and the boarded-up cottage in the swamp. What did these things mean? In school we were led down to the river of literary symbolism and taught to drink. I might apply the fictional *Ethan Frome* or *Our Town* templates to Buckminster and make up a story or I could stick around and ask questions: *Why was the cottage boarded up?* Five years after my first visit, I broke my resolve not to ask personal questions. But I did so by proxy.

"He won't let me in," I told Wendy Kaminer, a lawyer and journalist friend, "and his excuses are varied... He'll say the door's collapsed, the ceiling's fallen in, and the floor is rotten, but it's more than that." I knew that Wendy, who was not handicapped by being either a collector or a repressed New Englander, could get to the bottom of this. "I buy whatever gives me an *idea*," I said as we traveled the final four miles on the narrow peninsula to Owls Head, and I extolled the merits of a skeletal toaster, reduced to a web of wire and isinglass (mica) slivers (originally used to reflect heat). *It is almost not a toaster.* By this time, I had realized that the best at Owls Head had often reached the outer limits of familiarity. The definition of a fetish as an object of obsession made sense to me now, although I did not want to *worship* the toaster, I just wanted to *own* it. Wendy and I became tangled in a philosophical discussion about the ideal Platonic object—was a single leg, for instance, still a chair?[2]

Buckminster emerged from his house. "Palm Beach for Golfers," his T-shirt proclaimed; "West Tenants Harbor Hardware Store," his cap. It was a hot day in Owls Head. Wendy wore a white boater's hat to shade her eyes from the sun. I made the introductions. Buckminster, eyes obscured by wire-rimmed glasses, greeted us in a guarded fashion. He had a grip strong enough to crack our fingers, I was certain, but his handshake was under control. Wendy greeted him in a firm but charming manner, smiling, saying little while I explained again—for I had prepared him for this event—that she would ask questions and record his answers and did he mind? He was obliged to say again *Yes, it's okay, no, I don't mind.* As if for an important newspaper interview, he had set aside the day for us. Wendy suggested that they talk in my car, out of the sun. Making a comment about how *this* wasn't as full of stuff as some of his are—"Well, not *yet* anyway "—Buckminster hopped in and I wandered off.

At first I stood with my back to the road to study the lay of the land as if contemplating the map on the endpapers of an adventure book. I looked beyond the mountains of tens of thousands of battered household objects and industrial metal to establish the relative positions of Buckminster's buildings. Singling them out from between the metallic mountains was like trying to locate civilized outposts in a world given over to geological upheaval. When my husband, Dennis, first saw the place, he was startled at the dominance of these close-set lava-like peaks that reminded him, he said, of "a singular geothermal event."

Buckminster's own house stood on the edge of a hill. Following New England custom he did not use the entrance that faced the road but preferred to enter on the "dooryard" side where one or more of his cars was always stalled among a sea of scrap. At the end of this dooryard, almost buried by piles of wire, was a one-room work shed, the door braced shut and bolted. Beside the shed, the writhing heap of electrical bits soared ten feet high and twelve across, supported on the north side by the wall of the antiques shop and the DANGER OF ELECTROCUTION sign posted midway up the mound. On the other side of the shop was the corridor of plumbing Dennis and I had come to call Pipe Gulch, and, next to that, the aluminum mound that covered the side yard.

Behind the shop, in a large depression of brush, was a pitfall of copper and, off to the side, the chimney from a tugboat, fishing nets, and broken glass. Here too was the outhouse built in the 1870s—jammed with teapots, fuel cans, coils of roofing shingles, and highway signs. To the left of where I stood, beyond the spruce trees and over the lobster traps, I saw the edge of a third house. I ducked under the low boughs and climbed the aluminum pile to look toward the three-story barn. Behind the barn, by a panel truck used for storage, were several collapsing chicken coops, metal filing cabinets braced by pine trees, stacks of lumber, and a field of outboard motors—treacherous blades and steel ledges under the meadow grass. I climbed down and tripped over a buried bucket of mud, its brim flush to the surface of the ground. I did not fall. Now, some years into this odyssey, I had learned to negotiate the ground like a cat, one foot in the front of the other; I had learned to extract limbs from unseen traps but also knew well the shock of plunging in and out of holes. Particularly treacherous was the slope of miscellaneous harness and tractor hardware, bedsprings, and iron stoves.

Buckminster had—at least—sorted the metal into categories according to type: iron, copper, aluminum, lead, and zinc. The stacks rose in haphazard segments as if torn from a larger matrix. Walking across the castoffs of aluminum, I kicked crushed saucepans, Primus stoves, lawn furniture, ironing boards, toasters, irons, barrels, pipes, sieves, switches, dials, and wiring, torn apart like a factory following an explosion or a house after a tornado. Nor was this mountain pure. Many feet below, yet above the ground, I saw a layer of iron, like a vein through ancient rock, making a lateral shelf through the lighter elements, as from an age long gone. It's as if the top layers of the earth were made of pots and pans, burned, squeezed, and pulverized into singular, never-before-seen forms. Digging locally, I threw potential treasure twenty feet down the slope aiming each toss toward a single target to retrieve at the end of the day. Whatever I hurl might vanish. If I find it twice, it must be good.

I spend most of my life surrounded by man-made objects. I am familiar with the surface of *things*. To find them embedded in the natural world was a newfound pleasure—still—I had never seen so much stuff to which so much had happened. Fraying, tattered, cracked, flattened, swollen, dried, scrawny, collapsed, shredded, peeling, torn, warped, weathered, faded, bristling, moldy, clenched, tangled, punctured, battered, bashed-in, scooped-out, withered, engorged, trampled, toppled, crushed, bald, listing, leaning, twisting, hanging, buried, wedged, jammed, impaled, straggling, stretched, disjointed, disembowled, skinned, docked, gnawed, entrenched. Broken glass knotted to the earth by tenacious weeds, stinging burrs smothering the paths, scaffolding wrenched between boulders or gaping loose, leaving the framework to dangle from the sky.

Buckminster and Wendy sat in the car. "Call me Bill," he said, taking notice of our use of his full name, "or Bucky. Some call me Billy Buck."[3] Wendy asked how he'd gotten started in the business of accumulation and Buckminster blossomed into a natural raconteur. He told her that he had begun in the early 1950s and then gradually expanded, at first by buying a few windows to refit the antiques shop and then, because none was ever quite the right size, he kept on buying until he had hundreds of windows—so many that his pile became *the* resource for anyone for miles around looking for windows although he himself "never did find the right fit." Piles of these same windows with mossy streaks now buttressed the edges of major mounds, danced with doors and shutters across the landscape, and reclined, sodden among storm windows and thick casements too, in the woods against the trees. As an independent itinerant fishmonger, Buckminster had, in his words, "access to many attics"—attics he infiltrated in pursuit of small antiques and rags. Eventually he had accumulated thousands of pounds of rags, which he resold to be made into wiping cloths and paper. "When the market dropped I went through it all. I did find bits and pieces of homespun cloth, a couple of good quilts, and three or four nice little samplers. I had to hire a man to haul three tons of rags away. That business cost me money."

Buckminster's mother worked as a practical nurse. In the mid-fifties, when one of her patients had died, she was asked to dispose of the contents of his house. Buckminster and Helen helped her by taking in much of the old furniture. They began to attend estate sales and eventually opened their own business. While acquiring antiques, Buckminster developed a fondness for small iron trivets. He built a workshop, melted down copper and tin, and made pewter objects—match safes, spoons, and porringers—to sell to the summer people. He speculated in scrap and followed the market. He accumulated piles of used lumber and the canyon's worth of pipe fittings, "this, that, and the other thing…I'm the type of person who will not start a job until ten o'clock at night. And you can't go to the hardware store or the lumber yard at ten o'clock."

The hours passed. I approached Buckminster with a long steel pole wrapped in peeling brass. "What's this?" I asked. "Oh that," he said. "That's an example of my stupidity. Years ago I found an ornate brass bed stored on top of the antique shop. I guess I was buying newspapers and cardboard at the time." Needing room for these collections, he threw the bed out the window, where it became wedged between the outhouse and the trees. "Unfortunately it had belonged to my great-aunt Daisy—not my real aunt; she was everyone's Aunt Daisy—and it would be worth four or five hundred dollars today." After Buckminster deaccessioned the newspapers, the roof of the shop fell in. So much had been piled up against the front door, there was no way to reach the second floor in a traditional fashion, so he used a ladder and entered from above.

Helen and he kept a list of all the antiques they had acquired until her death in 1976, days after one of their forays into the vast realm of estate sales had delivered a mighty wave of everything-in-the-whole-wide-world to their door. The sales receipt on which Buckminster will transcribe an original merchant's code is a ritual left over from their antiques business. He no longer entered new items into the original ledger that contains the list of all their catalogued antiques, nor did he assign code numbers to objects that had none, yet his use of the word *inventory* seemed to embrace all his holdings. An accurate inventory of what he did own would run to many volumes.[4] At times, Buckminster would refer to errant scrap as though legitimized by code numbers and a catalogue—pound for pound, ton for ton. He priced the metal by weight according to the international commodities market, which he tracked, he said, in the *Wall Street Journal.*

I reinserted the post of Aunt Daisy's bed into its historical cleft between rock and tree, where it sagged against the scaffold erected to repair the roof that had recollapsed several years before. I could not find the rest of the bed. Perhaps there is a periodic suction that funnels all the objects up the stairs and out the top like a chimney blowing its stack. Overstimulated, I considered the possibility of hidden updrafts, vortexes, sinkholes, and tunnels. I pictured flashing lights rising from the nearby marshy ground and spontaneous combustion. The inanimate assumes new force; the invisible juices of nature overflow and pass through every available aperture. Stones ring, the sands sing, and deep in the grass late at night fifty outboard motors, long out of gas, kick in, drowning out the throbbing of the frogs.

As a piece of the world this place is small, but I will never see it all. As an adaptive strategy for understanding its (relative) immensity I take one thing at a time and concentrate on what I see. I found congealed slag from a hotel fire, a slurge of plumbing, glass, and stone, with the green patina of Minoan bronze; I found a rough file with half-moon teeth like the scales on the back of fish, a satin purse turned inside out into three pink, blatantly anatomical pouches, the top of a gas tank shaped like the hat of Asterix, the head of a broom like a piebald hedgehog, and dozens of humanoid pieces hacked from lead joints—a head, a torso, and stripped shreds like the muscles in an anatomical drawing from the Renaissance. Function follows form. As I walked along the side of the shop, selecting imitation body parts, the field of lead rolling under my shoes, ahistorical associations flew by and I was happy. A meandering course from thing to thing was the safe path through this place.

Wendy and Buckminster took a walk. They walked along the public right-of-way road toward the cemetery. He owned the woods on both sides of the road where old windows and doors leaned in casual profusion against the trees. He spoke of these architectural fragments, among them the spiral staircase, as being "in storage" and said that the situation was only temporary. "I mean I have as much respect for the cemetery as they do, my wife being out there." He had mentioned Helen several times that morning. "You must miss her," Wendy finally said. "I do, I do," he said softly, "I do. She died very suddenly. I mean that's quite a shock. If someone's sick, even for six months or a few years, you learn to live with it while it's happening perhaps, but when they go like that, it…you know, boom. You don't get over it easily. That's for sure…" He paused. "Foghorn's blowing." After a time, Wendy asked if he was still acquiring things. "Oh, I quit buying about four, three years ago," he said. "They don't like my situation. They just don't understand it. They think it's taking away from property values.

At the same time the land directly in back of my house here sold last year for nine thousand dollars an acre. That's a hell of a price for this area." Wendy asked who *they* are. "People like the Owls Head Garden Club. Better still, somebody who would decorate their wife's grave with plastic flowers... people of that sort, you know." His immediate neighbors have been very good, he told her. "It's usually someone who goes by once every six months who thinks the place is horrible. They work on various schemes to get me to clean it up. They had the fire marshal after me at one point. That was three years ago. That's the time I said, 'Heck this is it, I'm all done.' I'm sixty-five years old, sixty-six or sixty-two or whatever I am, and I don't need the hassle. So I just quit buying and agreed to clean up the best I could. You know it took me forty years to put it there; it might take me another forty years to get it out."

Wendy and Buckminster walked past the pond, over a lowland marshy patch, and uphill through the woods. Wendy later wrote that he had pointed out a hemlock he'd discovered as a child, "not with pride, but with a lingering sense of surprise." He traced the property line, recently surveyed, and declared, "I don't want what doesn't belong to me, I only want what I own." In the cemetery he showed her the mossy rock on which he had scratched his name, BILLY, when he was ten years old. Daisies grew beside the rock and here also, a few feet away, beside the granite gravestone: HELEN WORMWOOD BUCKMINSTER 1920–1976 and WILLIAM BUCKMINSTER 1922–. "My wife always liked daisies," he said. He could not find a stone urn he had placed behind the gravestone and pronounced it stolen. "The kind of person who would steal that is the kind of person who would steal from the Girl Scout Cookie fund." One of the older stones in the cemetery marks the graves of Chandler Farr, 1830–1917, a retired sea captain turned coachman, and his wife, Ann, postmistress of the original Owls Head Post Office. According to the inscription, Ann Farr was born in 1836, but there is no date for her demise. "I think she died in Connecticut," Buckminster said, "but maybe she is here. One thing I fear is that when I die no one will put down my date of death."

While they were away, I inspected the facades of the four larger buildings—peering into the windows of Buckminster's house, the three-story house that once belonged to another sea captain, the cottage by the pond, and the barn—their interiors off-limits to me. Nor could I enter Buckminster's house which featured the *cave canem* on the twin-paned door, but I saw that the curtains had disintegrated up to a few inches below their gathered tops and saw, too, the stacks of documents tied with string, bales of paper, and stray musical scores that blocked the downstairs windows. Trapped against the glass was a thin stencil with the words MAINE APPLES cut out in a curve of beaten copper. Over the years this stencil became a symbol to me, the thin edge of the wedge between gaining access and being denied. As a ritual before I'd leave for home, I would ask Buckminster, "You know, I'd like to *see* that stencil," which meant I wanted to *hold* it, and each time he said, "Well, first I'd have to take the window off—and the storm window too—and I can't do that."[5] And I knew not to ask him to lift out the stencil from *inside* the house.

I thrashed on. Rusted farm tools hung on the sides of the windowless sheds where silver shingles like darts continually break and slip into the grass. On all the larger buildings, recessed windows designed for a cold climate were cross-barred, the doors inset with modest ornamentation. Unrestrained, grass, roots, and tough briars encroached on every side, making it difficult to advance and harder yet to see. As it was, I saw so little at one time.

A broken mirror against a wall reflected a narrow piece of barn across the way. One door of the barn covered by a bright blue tarp braced by iron posts was extruding stuff. A hay rake, a pitchfork, and a baling hook were impaled at random in the grey walls like weapons in the side of a great beast. Back of the building Buckminster called the "captain's house" I peered through a window. Between the vines that grew inside and out and had turned this window into a year-round trellis, I saw bales of burlap tied with rope around immense vague forms. [6, 7]

The sense of mortality was all-pervasive inside this room; human generations had drifted in and out of here like so much fast-forwarded smoke and had left their furniture behind. Furniture will not evaporate as mortals do and, for some, old furniture and ruined things constitute the stuff of nightmares. Once my husband saw a couple arrive and go up the path to the antiques shop. The woman went inside but the man, halfway up the path, turned and *ran* back to the car. Through the broken glass of the captain's house, I smelled a deeper level of pervasive mold and saw fresh animal scat on the windowsill.[8] If I had wanted to, at this moment, I could have climbed inside.

Back from their walk, in the dooryard Buckminster was talking to Wendy about his family. The Posts, on his mother's side, settled the town of Owls Head around 1800. Buckminster grew up here as the middle child. His half sister and her children still lived nearby. He told Wendy about the death of his father when he was three, about his mother's long career as a nurse, and about his spinster aunt Susie, an itinerant schoolteacher for forty years, who took them in. He had lived in the same house since the age of four, which, along with the small cottage and the shop, he had inherited from Aunt Susie. Buckminster went to a one-room school just down the road and to high school in Rockland, five miles away. He walked forth and back from Owls Head almost every day. When tired of walking he would run—from one telephone pole to the next. He joined the track team and finished third best for the mile for the "class B schools" in the state of Maine. When I rejoined them they were absorbed in recording Buckminster's love of hockey and, especially, since the age of fourteen, of pool—both eight ball and nine ball. His pace along the autobiographical track was gathering steam.

In the fifties, when the local grange hall with its vestigial Masonic rites became a kind of historical museum, the Buckminsters went to a couple of meetings. At the second meeting a man said to him, "Well *you* ought to know about the value of antiques…." "Well," said Buckminster, "I didn't like his tone of voice, I don't necessarily know the value of antiques, and I don't like people thinking I do. Never went to another meeting. I don't know why," he added, "they call it a *grange*. The building was originally a schoolhouse and then a town hall … A grange is meant for farmers," he said. "Well, there aren't any small farmers anymore, only fishermen. They call themselves *farmers of the sea* and they use the building to play musical chairs and so forth. A grange has no business on the clam flats." In any case he wouldn't join any organization that didn't have a pool table.

His devotion to pool remains all-absorbing. "I was lucky I managed to graduate. I played pool...worked at the Bath Iron Works for a year...played pool. Then I went to Providence, Rhode Island, to work in the Kaiser shipyard and I played pool there, too. Finally the armed services caught up with me. It took three draft boards to nail me. I was in the navy for two years and then the war came to an end." He spent the second year in Honolulu on submarine duty where he played pool every day. Back north, stationed in New London, he met Helen on a train. He began to hitchhike regularly from Connecticut to Saco, Maine, to see her. They married but had no children. He gave up the game for twenty-five years for the sake of marital harmony. He labored for seven years at a fish factory, as a door-to-door fishmonger, as a metalsmith. He sold newspapers, rags, and scrap metal, and at night played semiprofessional ice hockey.

Since Helen's death he goes out almost every night looking for a tournament (eight ball) or a game of nine ball. He drives all over the state. "Last night to Belfast, the night before to Portland, and tonight I go to Bridgton, about nine or ten miles this side of the New Hampshire border. I gamble—I lose—I win." It is clearly all the same to him. "Some guys have never heard the expression *it's how you play the game.* I've had guys break cue sticks across the table. Never over my head, fortunately."

A philosopher in the pool hall, Buckminster was less tolerant of customers. There were fewer visitors now. "The place has deteriorated some, I guess," he said. "Things have grown up here a lot so that perhaps people can't see the sign. I don't know what the story is...I usually sleep until eleven or twelve because you know if you get home at three what are you going to do? You gotta sleep sometime. I'm sure I've missed a few customers but after forty years I just can't handle it." Wendy asked him why his customers irritate him so. "Well, they try to beat me down for one thing," he said. "They look at my situation...and they think *this guy needs money badly.* Instead of being tactful and saying, 'Would you consider taking somewhat less for this?' they blurt out, before we even get started, how much they're going to give me...'I'll give you so much for that,' they say. They are not *giving* me anything— forget about it."

And make no mistake. He was not giving anything away either. He would never depend on the kindness of strangers; he expects they will be rude. Hence the absence of all come-hither, BARGAIN SALE signs, and the prevalence of NO TRESPASSING, GUARD DOG ON DUTY SIX DAYS OUT OF SEVEN—YOU GUESS WHICH ONES!, KEEP OFF—DANGER OF ELECTROCUTION, and the simple DANGER near his well. It's not that Buckminster minds making a sale; he just doesn't like customers.

The kinds of questions I wanted to ask him had less to do with his biography and more about what he thought of the phenomena and pressures caused by material tides, the mystery of transitional forms, and the passage of time. Because questions about *order, purpose, meaning* are so abstract, and because they are linked to this environment—a profoundly chaotic environment of his own making—they seemed inappropriate that day, even rude. I would have to tackle those questions, I thought, without his help. While I tend toward arm waving and excessive emotion, Buckminster's manner remained dry, courteous, reserved. I couldn't just ask, "So—what about swamp gas ghosts?" or, "Do you often think about the time-lapse of human generations?" before I knew his tolerance for the fanciful or the depth of his own curiosity in such matters. My own tolerance was shallow enough.

That day, with Wendy, we were grounded in a conventional fact-finding reality that included Buckminster's admission of how wonderful it felt to have the right supplies on hand: "Yesterday I was repairing a lawn mower, rummaging through a bunch of bolts someone had dumped out of a bucket...found just what I was looking for, a bolt and a nut."

When Styrofoam replaced wood in lobster traps and buoys, Buckminster acquired fifteen thousand obsolete buoys and stacks of traps. At one time he had, he said, the biggest pile of buoys in the world, a real showstopper for the tourists headed for the Owls Head lighthouse. That day I counted fewer than a hundred cracked and peeling triangles, ovals, squares, and cubes on the ground and underneath the foundation of the abandoned pewter shop.

Buckminster told Wendy he had begun to unload the bulk of all his holdings, in particular several tons from the outcroppings facing the main road, because they upset his critics most. "It's very, very difficult for me to go to the dump," he said.

Wendy asked what he thought of his artist customers, including me. "Every time they come along, it makes it harder for me to take things to the dump because of the kind of things they buy." "What kind of things?" "Well...wet books for one," he said. "What do you do with a wet book? Speaking of wet, my roofs are in very bad shape." Later, when I read Wendy's transcribed notes, my ears burned. "Nice gal," he said of my behavior as a customer. "So modret. When I first met her she was...one of the few who wanted to give me more than I asked for." If only he knew how immoderate was my appetite! I wanted to roll the rocks away from the X-shaped barriers across the doors, wrench out the nails, and climb inside—if the vines and raccoons can do it, I could break in too.

Buckminster brought out scrapbooks of family pictures and newspaper clippings. "Some people give me pictures, which is very nice, and some people stop and start taking pictures. I'm right there. They don't even ask me." He showed us a picture of his house when he and Helen first began. It was set off by a few good-looking chairs and a bare lawn. "This isn't too bad. I don't mind this one too much. Although I don't remember giving these people permission to take it. They should have asked, shouldn't they? And this one isn't too bad. Here's my place six or seven years ago." He read the caption: "*Lobster traps and buoys and a sea of assorted junk surround a crumbling building in Owls Head.* Well, I don't mind that so much. That's a pretty good description."

Buckminster was critical of most of what the papers had to say. He reads another caption: "Now here it says, *There is much charm in Owls Head like this secluded bay.* Now that isn't

Owls Head. I don't know where the hell it is. Owls Head never looked like that." Another picture, of his place: "*A somewhat untidy antique store.* Okay, so much for that. Now they didn't give me any credit at all for this. That kinda irked me. No credit at all ... no credit whatsoever." The headline of an editorially thorough description of Buckminster's scrap-metal business from the Rockland newspaper read *Owls Header Rides High on Sea of Culch.* "What kind of word is *that*?" he protested. "What kind of a word is *culch*?"[9]

We shared his indignation. "It is pretty here," Buckminster said. "I set all these trees out. Sometimes people slow down, look ... and all they see is junk. This is not just a junkyard." "But—what *is* a junkyard?" we ask. "A junkyard is one that specializes in scrap metal. But this is a *conglomerate*, a conglomerate of everything."

Buckminster returned to what was clearly a favorite topic— the nerve of some people. Someone had planted flowers in a couple of old toilet bowls and set them up on one of the tiny triangular town greens. "Now *that's* disgusting." These gardeners were the same people who criticized *him* for "messing up the landscape." If he chose, he says, "I could bring in a lumberman and strip the trees right back. It's what I *haven't* done that I'm proud of. I haven't ravaged the land ... I haven't hurt it ... I just messed it up a little bit."

Down to the finest detail, Buckminster recounted a particularly trying encounter he'd had only months before. "This guy parks in the middle of the road, preventing anyone else from pulling in or out. He leans out and asks, 'You got antiques?' I said, 'Yeah, I got a few antiques.' And I have. I happen to own the earliest existing brass foundry in the entire country. I consider it very much an antique. And I have other things I cherish, too. So, he looks around and he says, 'Well, I don't see any antiques. All I see is a bunch of junk,' he says...I don't know whether the guy was trying to irritate me or not. I didn't know him from a hole in the ground. I said, 'Look, mister, why don't you get the hell out of here.' Those were not the exact words I used but that's close enough for now." Buckminster's voice, when I play it back later on the tape recorder, sounds strained. Once he found a five-dollar bill rolled up in the keyhole and when he looked around he saw an indentation in the dirt where a valuable copper basin had stood. Customers are always a trial, upsetting boxes and barrels, removing objects when Buckminster is not at home, leaving only token amounts of money—removing hubcaps from the cars, then tossing them in the dirt; stealing the original wooden wheels off the old Dodge in the woods, good tools, the tops off salt and pepper shakers, his favorite hammer, and on and on and on.

"And what," Wendy asked, when he paused for breath, "is the foundry?"

"The Holy Grail," he answered.

The dooryard had become a kind of base camp where I would stack the treasures I had found, half of which, like a beachcomber run out of pockets, I would have to reject at the end of the day. It is also Buckminster's primary workshop, where he keeps the scale to weigh metal scrap and where, on a tablelike stump, he strips wire from plastic with a sharp knife. The yard is an outdoor parlor where we drank our mineral water and he his Mountain Dew and talked. Unlike other rural yards, there were no freestanding car seats to sit down on. We placed the paper memorabilia on the hood of the nearest car. "Do you know what's in this car?" Wendy asked. "No," he answered, "I stuffed it all in there when I was in a hurry, otherwise it wouldn't be in there. I would have taken it into the shop or into the house." "So it's a kind of storage closet?" "Right. I hesitate to open the doors."

I seized the opportunity. "I was going to ask you..." I said. "In a couple of the houses there's a lot of stuff up against the door. Is that because you've decided that really you don't want to go in there anymore? You want to make a blockade?" They both looked at me. "Blocking the doors off?" Buckminster asked. He seemed confused. Wendy shifted her attention to the picture album. Buckminster said he wanted to get things out of the weather. He said he had no other room. He said he was in a hurry and he opened the door and threw things in hoping to move them later, but that before he could, he'd thrown something else in on top. I knew, as soon as I asked it, that the question had sounded different from the ones Wendy had been asking because it had nothing to do with Buckminster's history. *Are you trying to make it impossible for others to go inside?* Implicit in this aggressive query was, of course, my own ambition as a scavenger. I longed for unconditional permission from Buckminster to go everywhere. "It's okay," he would say in a more perfect world, "you go wherever you want to look for whatever it is you think you need because that is why it is all here—it's here for you."[10]

As we were now deep into the archives of family ephemera, the conversation shifted from Buckminster's methods of storage to a prize piece of evidence he now held out for our inspection: a series of aerial views of the place taken by a summer resident pilot twelve years earlier, in 1976. I picked up one of the photos and took my time. It looked like a small swatch of earth history. A triangular smudging covered the eleven acres as if a tornado had touched down just inside the property line and clawed across the ground. Between the erupting piles of debris, as if by a miracle, the grey wooden houses and barn are intact.

As I looked closer I saw a kind of stem-to-stern order to the clutter, as in a harbor where each boat has its mooring. The white wormy shapes in the foreground like a flock of tightly penned sheep must represent most of the thousands of lobster buoys. I was happy to see this view of the place taken before I saw it from the ground: the pillowed stacks, the graded aluminum pile looming pale and as tall as the captain's house, a mountain of windows and doors, and a dark shadow between the antiques shop and another smaller hill that marks Pipe Gulch. I could make out three people on the porch and one lurking back by the gate—could be Buckminster. I saw the piles of lumber along the road leading to the cemetery. In the woods the boards resembled army tents. And, come to think of it, the stacked traps looked like the sandbags used in the trenches of World War One, the bundles like military stockpiles, the window frames and metal like a bomb-torn village. A suspension bridge and fence were under construction and vehicles associated with the project parked alongside the water like an army platoon constructing an emergency route. I *thought* I could see the platoon... Of course, "It's easier," wrote Flann O'Brien, "to believe in something that is not there."[11] Certainly I saw a bridge, or I saw a dam. "I built that dam," Buckminster said, breaking into my revery, "to keep pond water from running into the well and to make an ice rink."

As I held the aerial view at arm's length so that the mess created by humans receded into the grace of the dark ponds and woods of spruce and birch, I observed that the boundary line between Buckminster's property and the one next door was unmistakable, for on the neighbor's side the ground was bare. When I pointed out how abrupt was the transition between empty and full, Buckminster replied, "Well, I didn't want my neighbor to have to step over my stuff to get to his house."[12]

As I relinquished the aerial photograph, I felt an unassuaged longing for more. More evocations of where we were, more time and unbridled access to every hiding place. Over the course of that day, Wendy and Buckminster had produced a brief history of his life, too much data to fit onto a single specimen label, but then, as the curator of this archive, Buckminster required no such label. I had enough information about him now to keep me out of the fictional tides as I proceeded—like a predator, however benign—to penetrate his world.[13]

Not six months after the pilot had flown over Owls Head and taken those invaluable photos, Helen died. "He took the pictures when she was alive," Buckminster told us, "but didn't get them to me until afterward." Helen's death upset the balance forever after. Alone on the seesaw for the first time in thirty years, Buckminster hit the ground hard. He had much to manage with Helen gone—too much. He returned to the pool hall, and, for several years, he went every night. As he reshingled his roofs and watched the foundations turn to sand, animals gnawed and scrabbled at these foundations, ice and wind tore the frames of the houses apart, and the weather moved indoors. Whenever I suggested a visit in January, he'd point out, "But there's nothing colder than the inside of a barn in winter." Even before I had gained access to it, I knew that, of all barns, his would be the coldest.

3

DISINTEGRATION

absuit   Habitant
toute   de donner
Pais étrangers   Etranger
   oduit égale–   avoient
endent à
le nombres des Habi

                              autre
   de les den   es puif   ice et
ur de la nour   erable um
en Prendre de l'Etrep.   p
leur ancien. Celui-ci   l'e être
de debit, diminu d

                —text from termite-eaten French book

O NE SUMMER DAY I take the plane to Rockland and Buckminster picks me up at the airport in his blue Mazda. As we
drive the ten minutes back to his house, plastic bags stored in
the well behind the seats inflate and rise around us, floating
up like jellyfish to tap against our heads and arms. Ascending,

they obscure the windshield. As I flail about to bat them down, Buckminster drives on in high amusement. He has cause to rejoice. It's because he has cleaned so much *out* of his car that the bags are free to float. He laughs because such levitation is rare. I try to go with the shimmy and lurch of our journey but the lack of a governing hand makes me want to swim like mad for the opposite bank, climb onto higher ground. I claw at the windshield where the bags cling. We coast half blind all the way to his house, and when we stop the bags collapse.

A broken-down car turns into a storage bin by degrees. It goes in order, Buckminster says: the clock first; next, the odometer; the heater; and then, time after time, the transmission. When he finally decides that that car has had it, he fills the interior—of the Fairlane, the Sprite, the beach wagon—with as much as it will hold. The smaller stuffings, hinges, hooks, and ladies' handbags jam against the handles, tumble into cracks. Too bad if I see something inside one of these cars that I happen to covet. There is no mechanical claw inside, like the ones in glass boxes at the county fair that deliver up prizes from the inside out. The doors, too, are swollen shut. That morning, frustrated by my efforts to penetrate the cars, I quit and head off to the aluminum mountain.

Raking through an undifferentiated pile of scrap metal with thick-gloved fingers accustomed to setting camera controls and exercising other fine motor skills, my hands are as clumsy as county fair-game claws. If I retrieve an all-time prize, it might fall into a crevice, forever gone. High up, one foot in a roasting pan, the other on an oven grill, arms full of window blinds, eggbeaters, and forks, I cannot think big thoughts. Cut off from the ground, as if by water, I often have to choose between philosophical speculation and keeping my balance.

Yet what am I doing at the heart of trashland if not to have ideas? The gathering up of ruined kitchenware now seems more absurd than ever. An idea is not an eggbeater, a mosquito, or a foghorn. But perhaps an eggbeater is not always an *eggbeater* and a teapot that holds no water is deeper than you think.

As I stumble down, something twisted catches my eye: a weather vane with three of its compass points rusted to the east. Do three winds favor the east-stretching coast of Maine? The winds blow east across the pinnacles of trash. Down below I find a plaster dog and deer, with scaly snouts, half-dissolved into granulated slumps, six rusted fish knives welded to a grey-blue board, and a surge of melted pipes. I grab for gap-throated sleigh bells, squashed copper toilet-bowl floats, half a butter churn, hollow bowling pins, a limp table with crippled legs. Beyond the aluminum mountain and a silvery pile of Maine state license plates—some burned, others creased like metamorphic rock—lies a sloping graveyard of the sheared grey humanoid shapes. I exhume the frame of a typewriter, its vestigial hammers like the ribbings of an ancient echinoid. Where does the sea end? At what point does a manufactured object turn into an organism? Do objects *drown*? Do they ever possess a life—beyond batteries—that might be taken away? Is an object transmuted into another substance ever, like a fossil, turned from flesh and bone to stone? When does an inanimate object become worthy of a scientific name? I name the typewriter *Underwoodensis corrupta*, a close invertebrate cousin to an echinoid. Its appeal is purely visual, of course, but as this typewriter aspires to the same lofty class of object as the book-nest, it too comes from the place where metaphors are made.[1, 2]

Like a box that has no top, bottom, or sides, the name of a thing collapses as its details are effaced, and it becomes more malleable. Gutted flashlights, twisted joists, broken files, and newspaper-covered cement slabs once used as ballast for lobster traps—electricians, plumbers, carpenters, and fishermen would recognize the original purpose of each fragment. They would repair them if they could. Our grander national notion of utility, running ever counter to repair, presupposes obsolescence. I have chipped these things from the matrix of the almighty thingness of our all-American world and, as I did not stop to mourn their demise, why not revel now in the stages of their inevitable disintegration?

I come across shafts, cores, cones, crushed hollows. Lacking details that once gave each its unassailable identity, the pieces mysterious in dissolution are perfect now. I seize on them to stop the flow of entropy. For what each object had thus far lost will be imagination's gain. Wait too long and whatever enzymes that have attacked them would consume them altogether.[3]

Farther down the hill as if descending into the basin of a dried-up harbor, I find anchors, oars, propellers, free-floating portholes, a wooden skiff, a life-jacket stamped with the name and date of the ship, and an iron chain with rust-dissolved links, attached to a crippled ladder. Once hung over the side of a freighter, this ladder with stunted legs, like a sea mammal stranded on the shore, seems profoundly lost. Pierced metal from the sides of a merchant steamer cover the slope like overlapping plates created by the upheaval of the earth. Over the years I have hauled the plates away by the truckload and, back home, nailed them to the walls.

If one could take the measurements of the density of stuff and the surface area of each piece at Buckminster's, the geographical size of his property would be immense. The extent of the place, eleven acres, depends of course on its boundaries, but if you measure all the surfaces within these boundaries, it approaches the infinite. Buckminster's land, like the coastline of Maine, is slowly sinking and his number of objects shrinking; but paradoxically, even as he owns less, the ongoing disintegration of whatever remains contributes to the surface area, augmenting the overall measurements and hence acreage of his domain, every day. As the years went by, there was never less to see. And as human eyes are capable of focusing on only one piece of a heap at a time, my work at Buckminster's was never done. The overall field of awareness of two eyes working is not quite one hundred and eighty degrees. The area of actual resolution within which one can clearly identify an object is about two degrees. If only I had a fish-eye lens for eyes or a gazing globe from an ordinary garden. Even a single, simple glass of water collects a wider view than my eyes can manage but these reflected or refracted microcosms are illusionary geographies containing details both distorted and intangible.

A cooler eye—no matter how narrow its range—would neutralize this chaos. There is too much to consider; and to make things harder, too much occurs in living color. Color complicates the world, which is why the sky-reflecting aluminum—

like silver water and grey rock—is conducive to quieter deductions.[4]

Over the years, driven by the desire to make connections between material and nonmaterial elements, I have tried to develop a light touch. I cast casual looks at this pile or that so as to prevent the pitiful two-degree field of focus from locking in. I reach down and a one-of-a-kind hops into my hand. And another, and another. I have found a rich patch. I have no choice but to crawl like an insect over the ground. I wish I had an insect's eyes. Even the aerial photograph from Buckminster's album did not show it all. As a collector, I was goaded on by the anachronistic illusions in that photograph, antiques that might still exist as weathered acquisitions from World War One—tents, platoons. Like any source of signals from outer space much of what was visible in the photo was now long gone. Here on earth, the landscape and its battered containers—so tidy from the air—become both claustrophobic and chaotic. Extracting simplicity takes work. When visiting Tokyo, a friend told me, she admired the commercial signs that reached "from the ground to the clouds" in a series of visionary towers. Because she reads no Japanese they soared as shapes without meaning, purely aesthetic. Literacy overwhelms vision. On the ground, I try not to read—*Almond Joy, Bitter Lemon, Salem Smokes*— otherwise I will never see beyond the promise of vivid tastes and odors into the center of things.

A coiling heap of grey conduit emerges near the base of a tree like aerial roots in a tropical swamp; paint curls in wide stripes like birch bark from a birdhouse made of pine. Nature winds round artifice: I find a plant thriving inside the hole of a hand-carved croquet mallet and a barnacle-covered bottle filled with earthworms. Inside the buildings, farm equipment lies tangled in lace; mice and squirrels have incorporated threads and needles from sewing baskets into nests or tunneled deep into the opulence of damp horsehair and straw. The traffic between creatures expiring and new life taking hold is brisk. Softened by the elements, objects crumble and inroads appear. I find fossil-like impressions in bricks, one as though an eel had fallen into the mud before it hardened, and another with the impression of cat paws—one print relaxed and the other splayed: the first step a mistake and the second a hasty retreat.

In a world where organic processes alter incessantly the contours of inorganic property, Buckminster applies taxonomic principles as best he can. He separates discolored insulation rubber from copper wiring with a sharp knife. He packs the gleaming wire in finical piles—it has taken months to work his way through these wires and, in recompense, when he turns them over to the recyclers, he will have earned, he figures, about 4 cents an hour.[5] He mounds purple mussel shells left over from dinner into woven bushel baskets and heaps of oxidized green forks and spoons into crates, tines protruding. The colors of mussels and flatware glow as if in evidence of an ancient ritual.

Buckminster has built a fence along the east side of his property out of faded shutters and random doors. At the bottom of the yard, in the mid-nineties, he bent branches into a garden gate buttressed on either side by slender piles of logs, as effective a barrier to intruders as a piece of filigree. "I like to cut a cord of wood before breakfast," he says, in preparation for the winter. These logs are beveled and stacked to fit. They point in one direction like dozens of the same breed of dog facing the wind. Across the top of each pile he has placed flat boards held down by rocks chosen for their curious shapes. These structures lining the cemetery road look more like roadside shrines or environmental art than like a winter's worth of firewood.

There is no sign, though, aside from his high standard for replicating ax cuts, that Buckminster is doing more than showing affection toward the natural world and getting by. He does not, as a self-conscious artist might, incorporate grander architectural elements into his structures, although iron gates, doors from a mansion, and the spiral staircase stand in the woods like pieces from an abandoned opera set. I imagine that the staircase came from a house from the Black Coast built by a merchant whose income came from selling slaves. Although he has often lamented the destruction of local historical buildings as described by journalists, Buckminster was unsentimental about the now moldy staircase and other architectural investments, which, in the near future, he was to sell.

In listening to several of the recorded conversations made over the years between Buckminster and me, I hear once in a while how his words are drowned out by birdsong. At the right time of year every handful of rust is extracted to the sounds of bird calls, every frozen lock to the shrill of spring peepers. The objects are still mysterious. If I recognize the original function in any single thing—to dig a ditch, pump gas, milk a cow—it is because I saw someone else using something like it once. I have never built a doghouse, chopped down a tree, hauled in lobster pots, or run an outboard motor. Which is why now I may see a stripped-down machine as a prototype for a new invention, a dream thing made from rubber bands and random springs, zapping with potential, yet tethered to the imagination of its inventor.

I pick up a window with a FIRE PROTECTION sticker. Silver, with a black-and-white profile of a handsome man with hat and hose, its adhesive holds the broken glass together. Like an eighteenth-century mirror, the metallic sticker has flaked into cells that reflect as much as they obscure. The mosquitoes are thick as I pull the frame from its old leaf trough. I have seized upon it in a fit of appreciation for the ambiguity of windows and mirrors that neither protect nor reveal but suggest. Back home I fill the window frames and photograph the results. One of the first, *Window for Billy*, contains three things—wood frame, crumpled wire screening, and iridescent marbles. The three-dimensional maquette translates on film into two dimensions: the screen becomes a fogged web of glowing insects, or cocoons.[6]

I understand all too well the impulse to Joseph Cornell–box the world. Beyond a tropism for weathered surfaces and idealized microcosms, I share little of Cornell's vocabulary of lyric opera singers, celestial charts, and marbled papers. I admire his work but am wary of the romantic yearnings the constructions—so attractive—provoke in me. In the end, many of these boxes fill me with regrets. I turn away toward a closer observation of the teeming and intermingling between organic and inorganic forms, of what happens between the ice and the inner tube, the sun and a glass plate negative, the rain and a roadmap. Spiderwebs outlined in rain drops drape themselves over dark pots inviting comparison to strings of pearls or to the night sky, but as Owls Head is a place of tireless consumption, of active burial and renewal by mice, squirrels, bees, beetles, ants, and worms, phenomena such as strings of pearls are illusory, soon dissolved by the sun. The materials from Owls Head come from a world where lace and lyrics have been recycled into incubators and food for generations of animal life. I encounter layer upon layer of gnawed and masticated lumps—stuff that causes allergic reactions: wheezing, sneezing, and rashes—which are not necessarily the same afflictions that accompany romance.

In the zoology lab I observed dermestid beetles swarming over the flesh of a defrosted mountain lion and, in India, watched as vultures dipped their necks into the belly of a dead cow. Once, too, at Buckminster's I stood by as a red squirrel clawed its way through a stack of *National Geographic*s from the 1930s, transforming them from commodity into curiosity—no life to begin with, no death at the end. The mountain lion, as disarticulated bones, turned into pieces of smooth white sculpture and the cow became an empty vessel, an angry, buzzing bowl of hide. And in a wooden matchbox I found a nest of grey furze, red threads, and comic book fragments. Compared to the frenzy of dermestid beetles and the jostling of vultures, a mouse nibbling "Blondie" falls at the Beatrix Potter end of the scale.

For most of us, maggots are portents of our own corrupt-ibility. I remind myself that maggots do not spring full-blown from dead meat. I am a mother who had no fear of procreation, but I know that for others germination can be scary stuff. I had a herpetologist friend (since deceased) who specialized in the morphology of frogs and whose mother ruined his Christmas dinner by seating him next to his pregnant sister-in-law. The sight of her swollen belly "made me sick," he said; "I couldn't bear it."

Each machine-made object starts out as a replica of its own kind. As self-similar objects disintegrate, clones turn into fra-ternal twins, into kinships, into improbable pairs, into singular incarnations. The process of disintegration that reduces com-plex machinery to its fundamental crumbs is the inverse of the process of embryological development—from a gleaming brand-name toaster, say, to its wire skeleton to shadows of rust.

Sometimes the stages of an object's evolutionary sequence are in plain sight. Along the border of pines, a few yards from the swamp, lie heaps of bulbous green bottles, used as floats for fishing nets until discarded by fishermen and replaced first by wooden and then Styrofoam floats. I have found all stages of the morphological evolution of these floats, including three exam-ples of a rare *wooden* bottle shape, a synthesis of the old glass bottle form in wood, carved by a fisherman from Stonington, Maine, in the 1930s or '40s. Some inventions, I suppose, carry in themselves indelible aspects of earlier forms. Buckminster will not sell the wooden bottles. I decide against the green ones. I cannot, therefore, demonstrate the stages of the sequence as I see it, but, as possession may be ninety percent existential, whether I own the evidence or not does not, in this case, matter much.

The weather turns, and now in the front yard I see the abandoned aluminum lawn chairs, mowers, sewing machines, and other things, homely under the soaking rain. Below, though, I know that toxic seepings blend. Once deep in the pile of wire, I found crushed tubes of artists' paint oozing viscous pools over leaking batteries and gears: *Vermilion, Cadmium Red, Burnt Umber, Flake White, Naples Yellow*—their names evoking scenes of blood, fire, volcanoes. Poisonous, gorgeous, the paint mingled with oil leaked from engines, lethal copper powders stained the dirt, and threads of asbestos wrapped round roots. Under the earth, on the rocky ledge, the brilliance collects, unholy pools that seep into the ground and may never dissolve.

Over the years I learned that Buckminster was committed to new beginnings including certain purification rituals familiar to many Americans. At 8 A.M. on February 7, 1965, he woke up with a headache, threw away his last cigarette, went down to the swamp, and yanked out all the trees. This cold-turkey remedy worked, for, "with the trunk of an alder in my hands, there was no room for a cigarette." Buckminster then built a dam, filled the pond, and as soon as it froze took to the ice. He rigged up strings of 300-watt bulbs on twenty poles, and a ragtag group of men and boys joined in the nighttime games. Buckminster, who had skated all his life, emerged from swamp-ice practice to join the Seahawks, an aspring hockey team from Knox County made up of "anywhere from swamp skaters to college hockey players," for whom he played right wing until the age of sixty-five.

Down at the Owls Head corner store, in the late nineties, I shared a table with a man who as a child had watched the night games on Buckminster's rink. He told me that the players concocted their uniforms from whatever came to hand. The goalie, strapped into football gear, wore either a trench coat or a bathrobe. There was still a lot of sports equipment around Buckminster's place—sticks and skates and football pads. Some of the skates—slim platforms with tattered straps—date from the nineteenth century. These players, of course, wore modern skates. But until I realized that their equipment came as close as money permitted to the real thing, I had imagined a bunch of Tweedledum loonies, with pots as helmets, using pot lids for pucks.

Where are they now, I wonder, those men and boys? Isn't it time they reclaimed these things? Couldn't the team stop by and help clean up this mess? But if, in this unlikely scenario, everyone who did own stuff here were to return, there would be such a crowd. I can see it now, as in a Stanley Spencer painting of a cemetery in which ordinary folk dressed in daily attire rise from their graves—all at once. They'd enter the shop, one at a time or family by family, to reclaim their things:

"That's my puck . . ."

". . . and raincoat . . ."

"I've come for the goal post."

"Hand over that hockey stick."

". . . My brother's goalie pads!"

"Her husband's bathrobe."

One day, cruising through the field of outboard motors, I found myself at the back end of an engineless delivery van. I climbed moss-covered steps and pried open the door. Expecting to find the same kind of undifferentiated overload as in the other closet-cars, I saw instead a spare arrangement consisting of two chairs, a table, and a floor lamp, all at such precise angles one could almost detect the chalk marks left by a stage manager. What manner of vagrant had set up this room? "Must be by chance," Buckminster said when I asked him. By chance? I wondered. Whoever placed the armchair on the left, the straight-back on the right, and the table in between was not just *dumping* furniture; he or she was *making plans*, a stab at a new beginning. There were no outlets for the lamp and the frayed cord hung in space. So, with the door closed, all cogitation in a comfortable chair would have to go on in the dark—with a limited supply of oxygen.

Several years later, between two boulders by the old outhouse, I caught sight of a waterfall—it twisted, it glinted, but did not move. I took a closer look. No—it was not water but a cascade composed of hundreds and hundreds of flip-top rings from cans of Mountain Dew. That day I photographed Buckminster's laundry line. He often hangs out T-shirts and a rag or two, sometimes a pair of chinos or a few socks. Once he included a dirty silk handkerchief commemorating friendship between soldiers from Camp Atterbury in Indiana. I purchased this right off the line and at home made the mistake of running it through the DELICATE cycle of the washing machine, which all but obliterated the message: *My Friend—In these troubled times / It's good to be sure / That friendships like ours / Will always endure / The future may send us / The heaviest weather / But we'll see it through / If we just stick together.* Today, Buckminster had presented a variation on the classic domestic clothesline: four plastic bags and a dirty sock. "I do so like to show a fine wash," he said.

I continue to collect objects notable for their exquisite reductions and patinas. Within this category of the *sublimely diminished* (as generous a group as that of the arthropods, which includes both lobsters and beetles) are things bereft of their original potential, yet still familiar: a bird cage flattened into interlocking parallelograms, rubber and copper printers plates stuck together in self-imprinting stacks, test tubes packed into corrugated cardboard sleeves warped into six-sided honeycomb cells, and indoor carpet left outside and now slimy as kelp. As I had no wish to own this carpet, I used it in situ as background in photographing a group of funeral flower baskets.

I have gathered up books in all phases of decay. They run the gamut from gently weather-beaten to hard-core metamorphosed, from faded volumes that can—more or less—be deciphered to books that resemble shells and rocks, and, beyond, to rocks that look like books. I find a poetry book unfurled to the rain. It has a clotted look, like wet wool, as words, letters, and syllables swell. Some words are now elongated, some lines swung around ninety degrees. Verses slide away under the rain, dragged by the weight of the paper into gullies and pulp dikes. The book slumps to the touch, malleable as clay, its lines broken in half, with crooked *J*s and *L*s, mushed *M*s, *T*s, and independent commas. Liberated letters gather like the limbs of insects at the base of the churned up embankments and as the

book dries, real insects—silverfish, sow bugs, and very tiny ants—
will join them. The poems metamorphose into concrete poems,
the original strophes transformed into a cryptic warp and drift
of paper and ink.

I buy hundreds of things. I load up my truck with boxes
and bales that creak against the roof. Back home I store them
in my studio. Perhaps I will experience a flash of understanding and reinvent these damaged goods as idealized objects, as
hypothetical tools from a long-forgotten civilization, a collection of props for a Doomsday stage, or, simply, as a friable collection of debatable beauty. Until I establish some kind of order,
of course, it is all just trash.

Unless I came up with a rare tool, an overlooked Post family artifact, letters from the Civil War, or papers concerning
his foundry, a bemused Buckminster continued to sell me almost
everything I wanted. After several years, he got the drift of
my intentions, and by the early nineties he began to set aside
likely candidates. Each time he remembered only that he had
done so—not what or where. Once, under thin strips of carefully
cut rubber I found a cache: miniature lead figures, all but one
beheaded: riders, horses, and foot soldiers. One of these, the
upper half and head of a horse, looked like an ancient Chinese
stallion, and all as though they had come from an exotic tomb.
In turning the broken figures out of the soil and protecting
them like abandoned children under a convenient cabbage leaf,
Buckminster, as the deity of this place, had manifested his true
benevolence. I took them gratefully and, on a later trip, I bought
the strips of rubber, too. Buckminster had rescued the rubber,
originally from car tires from his pond, where swollen by water

and contracted by ice they had warped over the years into psy-
chedelic ribbons or snakes that had, in systematic fashion, swallowed one plump rodent after another but had not yet digested
them.

"Let's face it," Buckminster had said to Wendy, now more
than ten years ago, "the kind of thing she buys, I would take to
the dump." But that was then. When in 1996 I find a battered
photo album just inside the threshold of the front door, I know
that he has left it there for me to find because he, of all people,
understands my preferences. The album is so beaten by decay
that only a few details remain in the emulsion that curls up
from the black paper like strands of seaweed.[7]

Rarely, if ever, do I learn an object's actual history. I do not
know who wore it, sawed with it, cut with it, rode it, cared for it,
broke it. If there are initials on the blade or handle or flyleaf,
there is a danger Buckminster will catch a whiff of provenance
and refuse to sell. Usually, I do not care. I am after the butt ends
after all—the fact-free, provenance-lacking, bucket-kicking,
burnt-out, no-good nameless shard that, in passing, just happens to look like something else.

I pick up certain things I think I've seen before. Under the
rubble, I find the same brand of flashlight or thermometer my
family owned. I turn on the flashlight and the beam flickers.
The mercury under the glass on the rusted thermometer is,
by some miracle, intact.

I find a broken toy, a tin boy riding a tricycle. The boy has
fallen off the pommel seat, his right upper thigh has rusted away,
but his feet are firmly riveted to the pedals. Like an unauthorized
replica of the sweet-faced boy doll from the animated film by

the Brothers Quay based on Bruno Schulz's *Street of Crocodiles*, I recognize him instantly. In buying him, I buy him back. Sometimes I still dream that I'm riding a tricycle. There's more to this toy, though, than a souvenir or a personal avatar—what is it then? Oh yes, something *happened* with freakishness when I was five, and flashing back I find the boy and the tricycle— embedded in the past like a pin.

This boy is like the boy with the missing fingers I met when we were both four. I noticed his hands for the first time as we rode our bikes side by side over a rough sidewalk. My mind struggled to restore the proper number of fingers to each of his hands, but he must have been tricking me, because they were not there. Were they caught inside his hand? I gave up; it was too much of a problem. I could not fix it. I pedaled fast out in front, veering to the outer edge of the sidewalk, until he realized that I was making a getaway. "Hey! Hey!" he called as I clattered off, back to Grandma on the front porch, and to a nest that, so far, had included not a whisper of the missing, maimed, or misbegotten.

4

DIGGING DEEPER

In the olden times, many, many millions of years agone—
folks wrote on "bricks"... tomes in brick, news in brick,
songs in brick ... poems in brick, love letters in brick.
　　　　　　—George Herriman, "Love Letters in
　　　　　　　　Ancient Brick," *Krazy and Ignatz*

BUCKMINSTER IS ALMOST always obliging. If I were to ask him for the chassis of that 1922 Dodge at the edge of the backyard, I know that he would try to dig it out. The car, converted into a tractor, stopped functioning when the spokes fell off the original wooden wheels. Those wheels were filched years ago. Buckminster found eight dollars and a note, "This should be enough," pinned to his door.

Little remains of the dashboard, engine, or frame, now a rooted wreck open to the trees and sky. One day I pulled on the inner tube that coiled around a tire rim and the rubber slithered out like a sleepy snake, turquoise, crackled, a ribbon of loveliness. I put it in my sack. I will show it to him later. I turn my pockets inside out several times each visit, declaring every nail.

One day, in the late eighties, I enlisted his help in pulling a horse's bridle and harness out of a small hill used by the local blacksmith a hundred years before as a dump. Buckminster had already mined the site for antique horseshoes and bottles silvered by minerals in the soil. He took a pickax and chopped in and around the roots of a pine tree he had planted years ago on the top of the mound. "This tree will fall on me someday," he said. I suggested he cut it down before digging beneath it. "Now that's a good idea," he said and he laughed. The horse's harness sprawled downward and, like the roots of a tree, had grown around stones and hardened earth. I tugged on one uprooted end and then on another, thinking *If I pull hard enough, I will wrench the skeleton of the horse from the ground.*

As a small boy, Buckminster remembered digging in his aunt's flower garden, but as a man he has had to work in the dirt for practical reasons: to dig a ditch, construct an embankment, or excavate a new well. I've never had to dig from necessity, only from curiosity. As we dig around the harness we unearth hill-embedded back end of the box I had thought was a child's coffin. "For tools," he says.

As the shovel scrapes deeper into the base of the mound, we find no organic evidence of fish, human, or horse—not even those thicker bits, of skulls and teeth, which, underground, hold out longer against decay. Dark earth is mixed with sand and ash and shell. The ash pours from cracks in the sand and the sand remains light in color, resisting the mud. We uncover clay-encrusted tin cans, bottles, and stained clamshells. The same kinds of roots, ashy soil, and shells occur all up and down the coast of Maine, wherever earlier people had built fires, eaten meals, and generated refuse. Buckminster says there is one such ancient midden in Damariscotta—a wall, over fifteen feet high and two hundred feet long, of compacted oyster shells.[1] He shifts his shovel to the top of the mound. I wonder if the ribs of the horse will come up clean as ivory. I would prefer not to see the flesh—or a still-live predator chomping on it.[2] I imagined the horse's backbone attached to the bridle facing down inside the hill, its ribs filled with this unyielding clay. But until you have the evidence, of course, you just don't know. Perhaps the bridle and reins are holding an enormous rock in place. Not long before, I had read of ancient people tethering a meteorite to the ground so that it would not, like a restless animal, escape. When the reins do emerge from the compacted earth they come up without bones, without rocks—extraterrestrial or otherwise—but they do still smell of horse.[3]

In the end, preferring what I thought was down there to what we had disinterred, I decide not to buy the harness after all. Buckminster doesn't mind. Over the years, he has endured these moments of fickle enthusiasm without much comment. He doesn't mind the digging; we've had some fun. His strategy as a merchant remains unclear to me. Once he said that if he were to paint everything blue he'd make a fortune. A claw-foot bathtub painted wagon wheel blue and perhaps used as a drinking trough for the cows sold for more money than he anticipated. "They like blue things," he says. "I see what you're saying," he nods, when I extol the beauty of weathered things, but he never charges more for beauty.

Most rural dumping grounds contain wrecked cars. At Buckminster's there are only five: his three "storage cars," the panel truck, and the old Dodge. In the tall grass I used to stumble on steel hood ornaments discontinued in the fifties as potential lethal weapons: streamlined sprites from the Packard, Indian heads from the Pontiac, and sleek airplanes from the Oldsmobile. I found a child's pedal car, passenger side consumed by burial in pine needles, with blue painted grille and pedals hanging on like flippers underneath. For many years Buckminster had a collection of hubcaps, radiators, and "cooler heaters" taken from larger defunct cars picked clean by scavengers before they were dumped into the deep water of nearby granite or limestone quarries. I asked him if he thought the cars were still down there, and he said, why not—"hundreds of them"—and if you dove thirty feet down, he said, "You'd probably come up with some good 1957 Chevys." Groundwater fills the rock craters abandoned by mining companies as surely as it fills a well. I asked Buckminster if he had ever swum in the quarries and he said no, that they were full of eels that have migrated from the Sargasso Sea. He said that the eels, cushioned in their slime, travel to inland waters. They are also found in reservoirs, and one year when his small pond dried out he counted a dozen heads sticking out of the mud.

At times Buckminster flashes an X ray–like memory. One day, he tells me that new kiln grates, used to process limestone from the nearby quarry in Thomaston, lie at the very bottom of the aluminum pile. And sure enough, fifteen years later, when tons of aluminum were hauled away, the grates emerged unscathed, precisely where he said they'd be. The Dragon

Cement Company on the edge of Rockland, a pale-silver kingdom featuring steam-puffing towers, immense pits, and a splendid red dragon logo, is the descendant of the early coastal mining
industry. According to Buckminster, at one time Thomaston
boasted the "deepest mine in the world," dropping four hundred feet underground. Rockland, once known as Lime City,
now holds the most famous annual lobster festival in the state.
Which is why Buckminster once owned fifteen thousand buoys
and why he still has two walls and a slag heap of cement slabs
used as ballast for the wooden traps set out in Penobscot Bay.
Many of these molded oblongs are covered on one side with
palimpsests of faded newspaper and barnacles. The newspapers
had prevented the wet concrete from pouring out between the
slats of the traps. The exfoliating of the concrete along the edges
resembles pages that cannot be opened. The rough side of each
slab is incised with the lobsterman's surname, like that of an
author. The names are suggestive. Miller without the R, for
example, becomes *Mille*, for "thousand" and now the trap-weight
looks like a Roman milestone. With fragments of op-eds, obitu-
aries, and want ads stuck into cracks there is a booklike quality
to this collection. Pale stock-market indexes evoke lists from
other times: a catalogue of slaves in a ship off the coast of Ostia,
the number of locusts in the Egyptian plague, visible stars represented numerically.[4] I find the TV schedule: *Captain Kan-
garoo Showtime* runs throughout the morning. And, through
the ruins of an otherwise extinct narrative, a comic strip balloon:
"I can feel a tremendous pressure building up in my brain!"[5]

Whenever I ask Buckminster, "What is this?...what's this
for?" he turns it over in his good-sized hands: half a bowling

ball, a crucible, a hitching post. His hands are deeply seasoned and the wrinkles on his fingers dark. The most obtrusive feature a hardened lump on his fourth finger formed under the glove worn to strip miles of wire from tire treads. His shallow seashell fingernails have all broken to the quick. "A rack for seed packets"—he identifies the rusted staircase of small ledges—"seen better days...and this is the door to a Boston stove." He reads aloud, *Keep ashpit free from ashes*. I find disembodied brand names in embossed or imprinted metal, Honda, Zippo, Belvedere. I show Buckminster a three-branched metal arm capped with cups, which he identifies as an agitator for a commercial Easy washer. I drag out what looks like the shell of an iron lung, which he reclassifies as the bottom of a Crosley Icyball refrigerator (originally manufactured in Canada, he adds, and fashionable in the 1930s). A cone-shaped container turns out to be an exploded mortar shell from World War Two, and the hacked body shapes made of lead—stripped muscles, knees, helmet-shaped heads, and wrinkled torsos—major plumbing joints.

As a forensic specialist Buckminster excels at identifying the industrial pieces. He handles paper ephemera, playing cards, cigarette cards, and especially the less-damaged books with gentle curiosity, saying "huh, huh," as if he has never seen antique paper or books before. He treats much of his inventory as though it had appeared overnight from parts unknown and must be approached with respect and caution.

I have never seen him treat anything like trash, never seen him toss anything carelessly aside. I remembered now that I was in his kitchen the day he scraped bushels of flip-top rings from cans of Mountain Dew from the floor, separating them from screws and nails. He was ebullient as he applied his unsung talent for taxonomy to the chaos around him. "I live like a mole," he said, "and something I saw two days ago might now be a foot down." In the middle of the night, a shelf loaded with papers had crashed to the ground. "I guess the Scotch tape or electrical tape gave way...mostly income tax forms," he said. "But I thought a truck had hit the house...had quite a *job* getting around it. And," he added, "I don't want to end up like the Collyers." He tossed another bag of flip-tops onto the growing pile.[6]

When it comes to the classification of his wares, Buckminster weighs copper, tin, lead, or brass on a rusted scale equipped with a range of dome-shaped weights, and he charges the market value, but for every unticketed object he employs invisible scales from a hypothetical marketplace.[7] He does not know what he should ask. Nor do I suggest a price, ignorant as we both are of any guide that accounts for so much imperfection or might place a dollar value on decay.

Of certain benighted scraps Buckminster will say, "Let's call it miscellaneous." This is okay by me. At these delicate moments of the transfer of property, I do not want to hear too loud *the names of things*. The danger of too much scrutiny is that issues of history and provenance will promote mere lumps far beyond the significance they have for me as raw materials. Too much history may jinx the sale altogether. If a bent nail comes with the suspicion that it once had belonged to someone from a well-known family from Rockland, Buckminster will not sell it. Local history, he says. If he takes the nail out of circulation because it has now acquired the burden of provenance, my cause, in favor of the mutability of ruined things, is lost. Buckminster's ideas about pigeonholes include "somewhere safe like the kitchen table or the edge of that shelf." I am familiar with such methods of safekeeping and fear how doomed they are; I worry in time that he and the nail will drift apart. If it were mine, I would store it with other nails—safety in numbers. As if on a virtual wishbone Buckminster and I pull in two directions to see who gets to keep the nail.

In the late 1940s, for two years, my family lived in Madison, Wisconsin. Our house was at the bottom of an old Indian burial mound. Near that house once, a human skull washed downhill and became lodged in an outside drain. An official excavation took place and the skull was rescued. Inspired by rumors surrounding the event, and for several blissful hours, I rearranged the rock garden of the rented house, an activity that netted me a full day of incarceration in the bedroom. I doubt that at the age of six I was actively looking for human remains. The pleasure I felt in handling the rocks and roots helped me—not to a future as a gardener but as a rearranger.

In Owls Head, as far as Buckminster knows, the only disarticulated human bones lie in one or the other low-lying cemeteries. Fortunately, for the prurient, on his land there were imitation corpses—in miniature. Years ago he had inherited an oil tank full of a somewhat unsavory collection of dolls. He kept the tank on the far edge of his backyard until a customer he did not care for "came by once too many times," prompting him to haul the attraction to a less obvious place. I asked him where the cache might be. The dolls must be stranger now.

He said he did not remember. I felt uneasy and he seemed uneasy, as if my curiosity further compromised the dolls' inherent innocence.[8] In any case, they came to light around 1995, when a mound of car radiators was hauled away. Scattered in the oily leaves, plastered with dirt, lay dozens of naked plastic girl dolls, anatomically vague, with decisively painted shoes and socks. I found disembodied heads, one sporting a voice box in the back of her chicken-plucked skull.

One was made of rubber, now turning grey and creased like human skin. A powder of pulverized foam leaked through the larger cracks. Bones, not flesh, survive the decomposition of a natural body, and naturally, dolls have no bones.[9] But the surface of this doll had acquired such blemishes and abrasions that, for one stomach-lurching moment, she seemed as real to me as a murdered child. Her soft skin was marked by ellipses, hexagons, octagons, like the magnified cells of an exotic pox.

Restless with a glut of inanimate finds for which I would have to contrive fictional importance, I began to dig for dirt rather than in it. Digging for dirt means looking for human scandal, perhaps involving love or, at the very least, lust. I asked Buckminster for the history of the kept woman who, during the early thirties, lived in the cottage by the pond. I wanted the lowdown on the inhabitants of that miniature house once owned and moved from Crescent Beach to Owls Head by a rich man for his summertime mistress—a house known locally as the Birdhouse. I never got the same story of this liaison twice. Once Buckminster's nephew was present when I mentioned the Birdhouse and they winked at each

other in the complicity of men who *don't want to talk about it.*
It passed between them like a current. But only once. Buckminster did tell me that the girl "was a cute little lady," that
she and her mother (married to a sailor who went to sea for
months on end) lived off the road in an isolated spot, and that
one year they hired Buckminster to spend several nights a week
"to protect them against intruders." But he was the wrong boy
for the job. In his own bedroom he saw eyes shining out of the
darkness, like a wildcat. "May have been lights from the street,"
he said, "but I was afraid."

A year or so after Buckminster's dubious tenure as watchman, the affair of the Birdhouse began. There will always be a
Lorelei allure for me in any love story, spicy, smutty, unrequited.
Buckminster was now evasive as I darted in for details, steer-
ing a wide berth around whatever scandal there might have
been, as if around a bell buoy placed over dangerous shoals.[10]
How old was she? Who was he? "I want to protect her people,"
he said. "I was young at the time," he said, "don't know...I don't
know...can't remember." And finally, in a burst of inspiration,
"You know, her mother came to live there too." *Her mother?* The
tiny cottage might do for a single amorous couple, but the
mother too? It sounded to me like a French farce. "She had a
garden," Buckminster said, warming to this aspect of the story,
"down where the swamp is now."

I backed off. After all, as I have designated Buckminster
my primary source and as he stood witness to those times, he
must be in charge of the evidence. This time I will accept this
story, since he does—almost always—give me the same one
twice. In the story of the Birdhouse the players must remain

as shadows in the swamp. It is the wormy objects from this place that send down roots—their tendrils that drag at the heart.[II]

I remember the fluoroscope (X-ray machine) in the shoe store in Madison, where, on the way home from school, we would study our skeletal toes wriggling inside the shadows of our shoes. Every few weeks the owners of the store gave us prizes. Once the prize was a fabulous "all-day sucker," a ball of sugar candy made up of many layers. As each layer dissolved, not only the colors but the background would change from fields of polka dots to orbital circles or stripes. Flavors—lemon to raspberry to vanilla—rose ahead and then fell behind the geometric features. Unlike the fluoroscope where everything was revealed at once, the candy unveiled its mysteries one layer at a time. Anticipation, not appetite, egged me on. The thicker layers were to be *worked* through rather than relished; the goal was to see what would happen next. I took the candy out of my mouth every few minutes—or seconds—to study the changes, and in the sticky process something about the nature of time, past, present, and future, was sinking into my six-year-old mind.

By the mid-nineties Buckminster was hounded anew by the fire chief and the local EPA to clean up or else. As he hacked through the mountains and carted off the eroded tonnage, new cross sections came to light. The categories within each metallic group were established still—iron blades, wedges, blocks and tackle, zinc squares in tidy stacks, sewing machines laid end to end on the grass, and bedsprings tied to the ground by weeds. As the ground emerged from Buckminster's gargantuan effort to placate his critics, it was as if everything had been reduced to more elegant substances and basic elements: I came across marble slabs, lead sinkers, piles of old bricks, and small pieces of slate—the stuff of school. I remember in the eighth grade our English teacher's exquisite, almost Elizabethan script as she wrote the rules for diagramming sentences across the board. The dull dental-drill sound, the sharp *tac-tac* of the chalk for emphasis, the light shriek as she drew an arrow from one part of the sentence to another, all the expansive sounds of contact between slate and chalk linger on, which is more than I can say about the rules for the diagramming of a sentence. Her penmanship and performance betrayed a love beyond the teaching of language—the flourish of line revealed the soul of an artist, confusing, to my delight, the true purpose of the lesson.

Blackboard chalk, like the White Cliffs of Dover, is composed of millions of fossilized microscopic shells, algae, and single-celled animals called foraminifera. Lime comes from these calcareous nano-fossils that died on shallow ocean floors, forming beds of chalk. Under metamorphic pressure, compacted sediments in salt and fresh water turn into shale and slate. When I was a child, we used to roller-skate down sidewalks made of processed lime, draw squares for hopscotch, and write with chalk on brick and slate. When we drew on brick with chalk we dragged the exoskeletons of tiny animals across the surface of baked mud. So when my teacher took up chalk to write on slate in order to convey symbolically ideas about the English language, she was pressing creatures from an ocean against the bottom of a lake.

5

TRANSGRESSION

Timeo Danaos et dona ferentis–
[I fear the Greeks and the gifts they bear–]
—Laocoön to the natives of Troy,
of the wooden horse, in *Aeneid*

"Yep. She's one of my more modret customers," Buckminster remarked again to one of my friends. Tired of watching me burrow through the pile of electrical wire during a snowstorm, they had retreated into his house. I don't know how much irony that "modret" was dipped in. Always a gentleman, he gave my friend shelter. I did not have the time to follow them inside that day, and as he did not extend another invitation, the years drifted by before I was, for the first time, invited in.

The visit with Wendy had softened Buckminster's resolve to keep me out of the buildings. At my suggestion, we signed a legal form exempting him from liability in case of injury and one day, in the spring of 1991, carrying a camera and a tape recorder, I finally entered his house. I passed through a tunnel into what seemed like a cave, with several interior caves, which turned, as I negotiated the corners, into dim hollows. Buckminster sat at a high cluttered kitchen table in a pool of lamplight, like a medieval scholar in his study. As I began to penetrate the tunnels, I felt that I was moving away from the coziest part of a nest.

So full of stuff that walls rubbed against walls, in places almost closing the passageway, the windows were blocked, the rooms dark as closets. Materials that reshaped the contours of the four downstairs rooms served, too, to insulate the house. Sharp-angled objects poked out from every surface. What there was of the floor was worn to threads and in some places felt like packed dirt or stone. I say "felt like" because, even with a flashlight, I could scarcely see. I took some black-and-white pictures of Buckminster then, his forearm braced casually on a propane stove. The pictures came out blurred. Taking a lesson from Wendy, I turned on a tape recorder.

B: *It's hard to get through here. You have to be small.*
R: Definitely wall to wall.
Stuff keeps falling in around me. I go to pick up something and something else falls down. I spend half my time fighting gravity.
Lots of stuff.
I don't really want to live like this but I do so out of necessity.
Well, going through these papers could be pretty interesting someday.
Oh yeah. I go through all this stuff and I find things that—well, everyone in this business says it sounds good to say, "Oh he knows everything he's got and he knows just where it is." I don't.

Well...

I don't know.

How could you?

*I find things and I say, "Where the hell did that come from?" I
don't even remember.*

Then what do you do with it when you find it?

*Well, if it's good. I put it with the other stuff, I put it where I think I
will find it again. I write notes to myself all the time. Such and
such is... And if I move it I'm in trouble. If I move it I put a note.*

So in through here you have keys and papers and piles.

*Everything, everything... no rhyme or reason. I would like to get
organized. Those are all the postcards I've been going through.*

Wow.

*It isn't easy. That's my television. I'm afraid to turn it on in the
summer for fear it will blow up. The condensers get sweaty in
the winter.*

It's a little dark in here.

Someday I'll get it all organized.

It's a real uphill job.

It is.

... a big job.

*It is. You move something and where do you put it? I've got to
build a couple of small buildings... make a little room to sort
stuff better.*

The insulating tunnels kept the house cooler in the summer
and warmer in the winter but the rock ledge underneath also
transmitted the cold "like an ice cave." Buckminster makes his

meals on the fierce propane-burning stove, stoking the wood-stove in the cellar with logs from his own trees. Neither hermit nor aesthete, he goes into town every day to buy food, and out nights to play pool. His house is just his house. For me it opened new prospects where, as if underground, I lost track of magnetic north and the compass swung free.

Inside his house Buckminster was no longer merchant-historian but silent host, and I the avid guest. As I edged away from the kitchen and headed into the interior, he offered no advice and did not follow. I could not grab the ledges for support for they were not bricks and mortar but towers of many things unaffixed to one another. As a strategy for hiding treasures there may be no better solution than to amass them, heap upon heap, and pile them into towers too precarious to explore.[1] I made my way through the first two rooms plucking at phantom marvels and loosening the insulation with every poke.

As I pushed forward into the back rooms, I heard the muffled sounds of birds, trucks, hammers, and an ax as they boomeranged off surfaces of variable reflectivity. This burrow was not a single-point receptor for the daily sounds of Owls Head so much as a muffled thunder box. A crow cawed—under my feet. Now came a banging and dragging as if someone were struggling to lift the ragged copper and then the *thock-thonk* of the ax ever slower, insidious, seemingly chopping away at the pulp-filled core of the house itself. I gripped a grimy ledge for support. The sounds were more defined than any of the objects, shrouded as they were by each other and the gloom. At last the flashlight illuminated a classic metal horse, a perfect birdhouse, and an archetypal toy rubber roadster, each fashioned so that if I were to own just these three things, like three well-placed wishes, I'd ask for nothing more. The fact that I could barely see them fueled my desire to touch them, especially to hold the birdhouse, which seemed to be covered in blue milk paint. But how could I make an offer on the very lining of this nest?

The beam of light fell next on four shelves holding what looked like a deliberate collection: Aunt Jemima, snow globes from the Everglades and Atlantic City, a lead weight like a sea anemone, a china baseball from the head of a walking stick—a veritable constellation of what flea markets call "collectible smalls," which, while not exclusively decorative, possessed charm, if also, now and again, that fatal quality of cuteness. Propped against the wall was a formal photograph—apparition, really—of Helen Wormwood as a girl. Handsome to begin with, she was lovely here, endowed with the radiance of studio lighting. This corner seemed a shrine, though a nonsectarian, Down East kind of shrine. I backed away.[2]

As the amplified cacophony rose to fill whatever space remained in this twilit midmorning, I felt disoriented. I thought about the compass with three shafts frozen East, the shifting of magnetic North, of that New England earthquake long overdue, as I groped my way back to the kitchen table where Buckminster sat reading the real estate news.

"I thought so," he said, when he realized I'd returned. "That millionaire and his young wife have bought the store." He was referring to the small building fifty yards down the hill. I stood by, impatient, as he read aloud. "Must be my neighbor working on his barn," he said when I asked about the sounds dive-bombing his house. Having lost hearing in his left ear from his days of toiling as a welder without ear protection at the Bath Iron Works, Buckminster had heard only the hammer.

I remembered I had left the three hottest objects behind. Inviting him to come back with me, we reentered the jangle of gloom to inspect the highest shelf: the car, the horse, the house.

I am experienced with the bereavement of want denied. "I want gets nothing," our grandmother used to say, to teach us children how not to ask for treats—and, sure enough, the phrase "I want" lost us plenty. I used to run to the mirror to see if my crying came even close to mirroring the depths of the disappointment I suffered. But disappointment is more complex than tears. The image in the mirror looked like me, crying. Period. I still wonder how "want" looks. In the Victorian portrait studies of the human emotions, craven want is shown through narrowed eyes and a predatory expression. As Buckminster looked up at the shelf, I plucked at something irrelevant nearby. I felt my jaws tighten as he took down the car, inspected the horse. It has a price tag, plain as day. I tried not to look like a ridiculous Victorian. I even turned away in order to show that I cared less. Buckminster did not look at me; he was looking ever closer at the horse's hoofs. He takes his time.

This is the way he looks at everything I bring him. He will not part with history—except, of course, when he does. He turned the horse, house, and car over and over—it was driving me nuts. I decided to leave him to it, go back outside to breathe fresh air (it was raining now) and shake off frustration and greed.[3]

It felt like a game and I wanted to win; after all, doesn't the paying customer know best? I never want to haggle with Buckminster. I would pay him whatever he asked. So why wouldn't he just *sell* these things to me? As I walked, my weaker leg began to ache. For many years I've lived just this side of neurasthenia anyway, using the stamina that comes from anticipation and desire rather than from a natural physical prowess for climbing hills and burrowing into corners. As that energy drained, so did my hopes. It was dreary in this place. Everything was muddled and difficult, inaccessible, closing against my touch like a sensitive plant. I was bruised, I was bored. So now what? Who chose this Shangri-la anyway? When you get to the center, what, in fact, is there? I was afraid I already knew. "At a certain age," the world-weary secret agent George Smiley confides to up-and-coming spies at spy school, "we want the rolled-up parchment in the inmost room that tells us who runs our lives and why. The trouble is we're the people who know best that the inmost room is bare."[4]

I paced out my sorrow and much of the pain. It was hard, but as the rain brought out new colors in the scrap piles and added a whispering counterpoint to my walk, I remembered that it was not I who made up the rules. My husband said once that Buckminster, that tough, gnomelike figure pounding away at metal with a hammer, projected a Wagnerian force that reminded him of Alberich. I saw him too as a kind of deity from a Down East pantheon of gods that included the Lobster God, the God of the Outer Shoals, and the hardscrabble Potato

God. Buckminster is the god who presides over all great weathered copper and his standards—decency, moderation, and hard-
won effort—are invisibly encoded onto every surface. If I did
not play the game according to his rules there would be no
cache of soldiers under strips of rubber tire. I'd better watch my
step. I needed to have him on my side. I made discoveries in a
field sown by another. I congratulated myself on the brilliant
choices I had made so far, but hadn't Buckminster-Alberich
made these choices himself, load by load, in the first place?

Who said he was obliged to play the merchant from the
kitchen table? On the journey into the interior of his nest, I
may have hit at random on three objects that triggered personal memories for him—the way the boy on the tricycle did
for me. Most of my memories, like blind albino fish or spiders
that thrive in deep caves, come to light only when I go spelunk-
ing for them. My boy rides outside of the cave in plain sight,
an inseparable part of a personal inventory.

I breathe deep and go back inside. Buckminster sits at the
kitchen table. "Well, no," he says. "I believe I'll hold on to these."
He intended to keep them "high and dry," he said, to use as
models for castings when he reopens his pewter shop. I don't
see how that birdhouse will translate into pewter, but I think
I know why he is unwilling to part with it along with the car
and the horse—it's not for models but for love and it's no fair
asking to buy them.

6

UNDERGROUND

He was a man of one story; he had his cellar in his attic.
—Gaston Bachelard, *The Poetics of Space*

ONE HUNDRED AND fifty years ago, almost every resident was a captain, and Owls Head a busy harbor. Buckminster's third and biggest house was built in the mid-nineteenth century for Captain Francis Maddocks, retired seaman and, for some years, keeper of the Owls Head light. Maddocks resented his neighbor retired captain Chandler Farr for his habit of driving coach and horses across his property. Farr, who lived in what is now the antiques shop, resented Maddocks's driving across *his* land and their lives played out accordingly. "Two old sea captains...fighting it out," said Buckminster, the spirit of vendetta in his voice. The established cycle of trespass and feud passed on to the next generation. In 1947, Helen and Bill bought Maddocks's property as much for the right-of-way as for the house itself. "I wanted customers to be able to pull into *my own driveway,*" Buckminster said, aggrieved that to do so he had to buy a house. They eventually planned to live in this house but Helen died before they could make the move.[1]

There are porticoed mansions found up and down the coast of Maine, built from the proceeds of dealing in "black gold" (a euphemism for the slave trade), but as Maddocks traded in limestone, ice, and lumber, he had built a more modest country house not far from the harbors of Thomaston and Searsport. Since Buckminster acquired the house, the domestic functions of the rooms have been lost behind the bales and embankments. The back room is lined with shelves heavy with plastic and gilt presentation trophies presented at golf matches, basketball, bowling, and pool tournaments. The unengraved, unawarded collection conveys in its pristine state an air of contraband.[2] With fifty wide-bodied teakettles in the attic and mounds of magazines and documents gummed together by the damp, the house is a topsy-turvy repository. Except for built-in cabinets and a mantelpiece, none of the features of an inhabited house—parlor, kitchen sink, or grand piano—has been preserved. This is no house; it is more like a ship.

Two of the outside walls bow outward and, in the front, a ladderlike stair leads to a bedroom door measuring two feet wide, three and a half feet tall. The windowless cellar sits underneath a ledge of rock like the hold of a ship below the waterline. The only access, through a freshly dug passage with trenchlike walls, was blocked by a heap of small red rocks. In 1991, at the same time Buckminster and his nephew were digging this trench to redirect floodwater in the spring, they also laid a new floor inside a front room, which, for a few days, made the cellar accessible from above. I climbed down into this cave where the ceiling height began as low as two and a half feet (peaking at a generous five and a half at one end) and adjusted my eyes to the darkness. Cupboardlike hollows, scooped out from between and above the subterranean ledge like a pirate's lair, held a massive stash of silver-plate cups, bowls, teapots. Sounds from the outside, a truck, a dog barking, sonorous and dim, passed through the ground. Like a room in the city of Argia from Calvino's *Invisible Cities*, the air was earth. Fine grit filled my nose and lungs. It took willpower to leave the highest point (where I could stand upright) and stagger, ape-like, uphill to inspect the trophies with their papery skins.[3]

Not for the first time, I felt like a spelunker. Not a thief but a burrower, a mole, just passing through. Between the cellar and the road, organic changes proceed steadily. Directly through the ground about four feet up and fifty feet to the east, past ants and worms, silverfish, beetles, moles and fungi, the mouse had built its nest in *Flying Hostesses of the Air*.

Out beyond this dirt hole is of course all the rest of Maine, Vacationland, for more than a century dependent on the revenue brought in by tourists, especially along the tortuous coast and offshore islands from June through Labor Day. Owls Head boasts not only a famous lighthouse (built in 1826),[4] but also the popular Transportation Museum that features parades of old cars and air shows of antique biplanes. Although most tourists travel to Maine by car, the Rockland airport with many intercity flights a day is less than a mile from the museum and five from the lighthouse.

On the way to the lighthouse, no matter which road you take, you pass by Buckminster's. A host of artists, photographers, and tourists have come Buckminster's way. He has also had his share of celebrity customers, many during the 1960s, heyday of the fifteen thousand lobster buoys and Helen's antiques business. Andrew and Betsy Wyeth and the actor Robert Montgomery bought pewter spoons he had made in his shop. Louise Nevelson, a native, whose father ran a hotel in Rockland, came by for wooden scraps, and the actor Zero Mostel, allaround good guy, always stopped in on his way to and from Monhegan Island. Buckminster told me that one day Mostel came out of the back of the shop "to where the cash register would have been if we'd had a cash register, stuck a toy popgun in my ribs, and said, 'Okay Buckminster, this is a stickup!'"— a memory that to this day makes Buckminster laugh. Minutes after he's told the story, he laughs again. "Everyone has to have a gimmick," he said, somewhat wearily, when I asked what he thought of Andrew Wyeth. A native himself of the lace-curtain, dirt-floor seacoast culture depicted in Wyeth's paintings, Buckminster lives less than twenty miles from the painter's summer haunts. Of Wyeth's visit to him, Buckminster said, "I see him sitting on the steps of the shop blowing on a conch shell, then holding it to his ear... listening to the sound of the sea, I suppose. Don't know if he heard it, of course." He sounded skeptical as though remembering that at the time he had questioned the authenticity behind this gesture—of blowing into the shell. "He rode in on his father's coattails... and take that Helga," he said gathering steam, "the one he was supposed to be in love with... What baloney that was." When I ask for further impressions, he says that, oh well, Wyeth was "nice enough," but then, in an irritated aside, "that damn black cape."

"Not too many living artists can make it on their own," he went on, "but that's no reason to cut your ear off, like what's his name. I suppose he thought it was casting a shadow on his work."

Curious about why the artist would blow into the shell before holding it to his ear, I consulted my friend Richard Meryman, longtime observer and biographer of Andrew Wyeth. Dick reminded me that Wyeth believes that objects too have souls. "Shells have a tremendous emotional association for Wyeth," he said. *But what was he thinking about that shell?* I asked, aware that none but Wyeth would know for certain. "He may have been thinking," Dick said cautiously, " 'I'll blow a little wind into it and see if it speaks back to me.' "5

Buckminster's father, Thomas, was a distant cousin of the architectural innovator Buckminster Fuller, and in 1991, because of his genealogy, Buckminster was invited to a family reunion of Buckminsters from the eastern United States. He declined, telling me that the prospect of spending a weekend with strangers who happened to share the same name was reason enough not to make the journey. He never did meet the illustrious inventor of the geodesic dome and Dymaxion house, although once Helen and he "almost" went to hear him lecture at the Camden Public Library. I wish he *had* gone. Buckminster has, after all, at least one trait in common with Fuller, whose work was described by the architect Philip Johnson as having "nothing to do with architecture and all to do with dreams."6

Buckminster Fuller proclaimed his Dymaxion house "a machine for living in." Completely round, it was built to rotate

through the seasons with the sun as well as to provide protection against marauders, a feature William Buckminster might
appreciate in his own struggle against raccoons. Once, in imitation of mud houses he had seen in *National Geographic*, he
began (but did not finish) a rounded hut on the side of the
swamp, and in 2000 he erected a Quonset-shaped lean-to with
a roof of supple bowed sticks to protect his lawn mowers from
the snow. By spring, the lean-to had collapsed, as did Bucky
Fuller's first geodesic dome at Black Mountain.

Even in tranquil Owls Head, I sometimes wondered what kind
of bandit, hunkered down, might spring from a brackish corner. Once I heard howlings and out back watched as a tor-
mented man plunged cursing across the field of outboard motors.
He came up the hill, thrashing through jagged copper as through
dry leaves, and I was as frightened by this advancing figure as by
a rogue elephant driven mad by hormonal imbalance advancing on a peaceful village. He climbed closer, beating back the
demons as he came. He was mumbling and shouting—I didn't
know what—shouting and stumbling, his arms fighting for balance. I rushed to report the intrusion. "Him? Oh, he comes up
from Connecticut," Buckminster said and handed me a Mountain Dew, "a glomy kind of fella ..."[7]

Zero Mostel and madmen aside, most encounters with the
outside world erode Buckminster's faith in mankind, and he
expends valuable energy deriding the vanities and pretensions
of us all. One day, seeing one of his favorite bad guys, the fire
marshal, fishing—illegally—in his pond, he gave a well-reasoned

speech about the inconstancies shown by elected officials who impose rules on others, only to break them themselves, a speech that ended with the hope that an alligator would rise up from the water *now*. On another occasion, he came out waving a bit of tabloid news—a man had invested millions in grapes found frozen in the Arctic ice, grapes that might prove the existence of prehistoric vineyards. "And now what?" Buckminster's voice rose to a light keening, a mixture of indignation and sorrow. "He'd better find a freezer fast or he'll be stuck with a lot of grape juice." The day before, a member of the garden club had knocked on his door to complain once more about the appearance of his property, "And *she* was wearing a sleeveless blouse and shorts!" he lamented. "I mean, it's *October*." He is worn down by such encounters.

He expects, and sometimes receives, the worst. Once, in the mid-eighties, suspecting a series of larcenies that threatened to deplete his copper holdings, he rigged up an intercom so that he could "hear a car coming a quarter of a mile away." While the speaker stood free and clear in the bedroom, the microphone was partially buried in the yard. Whenever the wind picked up, Buckminster heard only the banging of pots and pans. But one windless night, hearing voices, he looked out on two men hauling copper down a narrow path, "out there in the moonlight—in the mother lode shuffling back and forth." He had time to load his gun. "I had one shot...only birdshot but they didn't know...one almost to the car, and the other ten feet out... And I said *Hold it or I'll shoot*—and I did." He caught one of the men. The sheriff caught the second one, and each received a fine and thirty days in jail.

One winter night, when Buckminster was on the road returning from a late game of pool, a thief broke into his house and pocketed antique coins and a valuable bracelet. Back home Buckminster saw tracks in the snow and the lock cut as if by a seasoned safecracker. "He could have pulled that lock off with his bare hands," he said, his voice rising. "But oh no, he had to *cut* it to maintain his reputation in front of his friends." In his bedroom, Buckminster found less valuable coins scattered. No one was asleep in Owls Head that night; snowmobiles racketed over fields and down the cemetery road. Suspecting the thief was out there "like a purse snatcher losing himself in a crowd," Buckminster called the sheriff, but the culprit was never caught. Taking revenge is one thing; recovering from vandalism another. "I think about that bracelet all the time," he said softly. "I kept it in the nightstand drawer... gold and enamel... it needed repairs..."

Of course, there were good days and fine customers. In the back room of the antiques shop one day, Helen came upon two men dressed like undertakers. They were urbane and very polite. She asked if they had a collection and heard one of them say, under his breath, "just the biggest collection in the world." Buckminster came into the shop and they got to talking. The visitors worked at the Smithsonian's Museum of American History and one was Silvio Bedini, the distinguished author of a number of articles and books on the history of scientific instruments. Now, not only did Buckminster own a book by Bedini, but he had read it. When he ran to the house and returned with it in hand, the author was surprised, Buckminster said, "to find it way down here, in the boonies. He went all to hell in a bucket and lost his composure, shouting, *He's got my book! He's got my book!*"[8]

Buckminster emerged sleepy-eyed when I arrived on an autumn day in 1998. He complained about the clouds and the disappointing size of his favorite silver-plumed grasses. Grouchy, he allowed as how the foliage would be rich this year. There were still signs of a full-blown summer under a recent rain, the lushest season I had ever seen in Owls Head: green leaves, heavy pine boughs, burrs attacking, high grass, flowers, mushrooms and toadstools in profusion, including *Amanita virosa*, angel of death.

"Did I show you the new well I'm digging?" Buckminster asked and took me out to the northwest edge of the land where a five-foot hole had filled with about forty inches of water. He had been working for days. As he was not qualified to blast through the ledge he'd now reached, he would have to stop and ask for help. One recent windy day, he said, he had almost drowned. While carrying a sheet of plywood, he had knelt to assess the progress of the seepage of water into the hole and the wood swung around in the wind, landing on his head, and forcing him down to the water. "I didn't go down into it," he said, but "it made me think."

Buckminster's original well, one hundred yards from this new hole, was covered by sun-bleached boards and topped by a faded red rag on a stick. From a distance it looked innocuous, more like a pencil drawing by Wyeth than a clear and present danger. The ground covered with thin timber cracked underfoot—*that hole might be anywhere*—and the stick holding the rag was exceedingly spindly. An area around a dangerous site takes up mental territory like the reddening around an injury, and over the years I had built up a litany of concerns: So where's the bull's-eye? Where's the abyss? Does a shaft ever shift? Does it have radiating fault lines? *Does it travel like a mole?*

I asked him to lead the way to the well. "Watch out for the small red ants... Bite? I guess they do." We thrashed through the grass and stepped onto the platform. It wobbled. He lifted the lid and we peered down. It was just a hole, three and a half feet wide, Ding Dong Dell—what's the big deal? He held up the bucket; of course it had a hole in it. I have felt like that bucket, not a bucket that goes down and comes up with potable water but one that has descended into unhealthy depths and comes back empty.

This well, dug around 1870 by Francis Maddocks, is twenty-two feet deep. In August 2001, I asked Buckminster how long he had drawn the water from the well and was startled when he said, "Until it went dry—about a week ago." (The well had lasted more than one hundred and thirty years!) He showed me two portraits taken around 1910—of Maddocks's enemy neighbor Chandler Farr, and of Farr's wife, Ann, both wearing snug clothes and button boots and both sitting on the box of a second well, down by the pond.[9]

Farr's well (now also Buckminster's) is only twelve feet deep. It draws on a spring originally used by Indians centuries ago, and later by generations of Buckminster's family. Even at the driest part of the driest year—1965—there was six feet of water in the well, enough at that time for three local families. Buckminster said that after about 1955 drawing on it had not been a good idea. For it was then that the fire department ruined the system by digging in the pond. Brackish water and salt from the road seeped into the shaft. Helen continued to cook with that well water and Buckminster believes that the infusion of salt contributed to her high blood pressure and sudden death. He buys bottled water now but prefers, as always, Mountain Dew.

Discouraged by thoughts of his disconnected yet never-ending labors, I found I was worrying about Buckminster. His gestures—with hammer or shovel—seemed as periodic as those of a mechanical workman clanking on and off the stage of an elaborate German clock. His ambition, to sustain and repair his property in traditional ways, seemed futile. As he buys spring water now, does he, nearing the age of eighty, really need to dig a new well? And like the blade of a windmill, the plywood pushing him down... Something was off about this visit. As I felt that it might just be that I was losing interest, I did not know exactly who or what was going off the rails.[10]

Only two weeks later, unable to stay away, I returned to Owls Head, and the amanita had shriveled. Some paths were lined and others covered with metal pieces, mostly red—a late summer garden made of iron.

For the two years between 1998 and 2000, Buckminster suffered from injuries received in a car accident after "some bird came all the way up from New Jersey for the express purpose of rear-ending me." Buckminster had stopped at the Owls Head stop sign, but the car behind him had not. "There was a can of Mountain Dew beside me. He hit the car so hard, I never found that can again. The plates said Virgin Islands, but he came from New Jersey." Buckminster saw the doctor several times that season because his neck hurt. Since the accident he's also had a permanent ache in his leg. The doctor finally prescribed an MRI. I asked him whether he had managed to relax during the test. "There was a picture of a damned raccoon right above the machine," Buckminster said. "What's relaxing about that?" The vertebrae in his neck, the doctor said, were beginning to deteriorate.

A year went by and I did not see Buckminster. But I kept in touch by phone. This was a hit-or-miss enterprise, as he rarely heard the ring. Once I called at 9:30 A.M. He sounded listless. It was snowing, he said, "colder than the inside of a barn...without the cows. Speaking of the barn," he said, "as though this weather weren't enough, a few of those boulders under the foundation of the barn have slipped from where they were supposed to be—goin' to have to fix that."

"I'm fair," he said when I asked how he was feeling. "I did too much yesterday...chopping wood." He gave an uninflected "yeah" when I said I hoped to visit. During an earlier call, in mid-sentence, his voice stumbled and stopped. Did we have a connection? For almost a minute I heard nothing. Then I heard him complete the sentence "...she said it was a coon cat but it was only black and white." I wondered whether I should complain to the telephone company or if he had simply told the first part of the story about the cat with his mouth held away from the receiver.

That year I felt my hopes drop. I could almost feel his weakness in my own bones. After the first snow I knew that Owls

Head would, for five more months, hold on to that chill. One January day, an ice film covered every pebble and my car spun off the road and into the woods. In the winter, I lurched around his dooryard like a stunned bear, my brain like a freezing engine block, all fluids listing toward hibernation.

The Rockland airport has expanded to include international flights from places like Galway and Brussels. Buckminster's schadenfreude knew no limits now when he spoke of the discomfort of the garden club ladies as they listen to the jets screaming overhead. As they have lobbied against the very sight of his property, let them now suffer that noise he will barely hear. While he rolls or doesn't roll the boulders back and forth beneath the barn, may they be tied like Prometheus to their million-dollar rocks by the sea.

7

PASSING THROUGH

I look into a dragonfly's eye
and see
the mountains over my shoulder.
—Issa, *The Sea and the Honeycomb,*
translated by Robert Bly

Once, as Buckminster and I were attempting to load a hay reaper into my car, an orange spider landed on his leathery arm and, fastening a line of silk, swung to the ground. I realized that our endeavor was about to be upstaged by something petite and bright. Buckminster held still as he began to report on the color, legs, and size of the spider, and then added in a tone of wonder, "Look! He's making a web!" while I, dehydrated, and exhausted from a day's worth of physical struggle, waited to see which—man or arthropod—would quit first. I was betting on the spider. The scene reminded me of the day my slender five-year-old brother, Jamie, in a bulky orange life jacket, had monopolized the attention of a famous writer.

My socially gifted parents had many distinguished friends, who had celebrity friends, and in their expansive gatherings we children—even into adulthood—almost always played a walk-on part. When I was nineteen and in college, at a family occasion on South Beach, Martha's Vineyard, Dorothy Parker was our special guest. Jamie, towheaded and tan, traveled like a bright bug through the dunes, absorbed in ambitious earthworks and doted upon for hours by the illustrious Miss Parker. She could not take her bleary eyes off my brother. Swaddled in dark clothes and propped in the sand at a right angle at—for her—the wrong time of day, Miss Parker's face was like chalk. She wore a wide-brimmed hat. Because I had read and loved her stories, I attempted to find now, in her appreciation of my brother, some hint of her splendid snake-in-the-grass wit. But, stunned perhaps into bliss by the drenching of sea air, "he's beautiful," was all she said, like a sentimental cuckoo, "so beautiful." It was as if she'd never seen a child before. And I, too, stunned—by the sight of this spectral genius gone to seed—wished nevertheless that she would show a flicker of interest in my own existence. I had hoped that, for just a minute, she would turn her filmy eyes my way, and ask me a question—anything that I might carry away and own forever: *And you? What are you excavating?*

Now, as the orange spider deliberated the current of the wind and Buckminster seemed content to accommodate its desires forever, I swayed under a load of copper. We had, in a sense, been mucking out the stable; my hands smelled of horses long gone. I balanced the load against the fender until the spider veered off and Buckminster came to the rescue.

Buckminster does not look to others for personal affirmation. Animals, birds, and insects, however, do exercise a kind of shamanistic power over him. They amuse him, but he also finds them capricious, destructive, and, above all, mysterious. He charts their ways with respect. He often told me the story about the two-hundred-pound red pig he kept as a pet when he was eleven. One day, when he was cleaning out his playhouse (which he had built and which measured not much bigger than the pig), the pig decided to join him. Beating her back with his broom, Buckminster managed to escape before she could smother him against the inside walls.

To this day, he excercises caution around all creatures. Yet the thoroughness with which he describes their ways is often tempered by affection. He handed over a car-squashed toad to me—tenderly. He spoke of crickets that chose to spend the winter in his stairwell as his companions. He told of grasshoppers hurling themselves against the outside walls of his house—*kamikaze*—for no apparent reason, and of blackbirds learning how to fly. The most destructive creature around the place? "Raccoons," he replied, aggrieved by the very thought. The raccoon (described by the Algonquan Indians as "he who digs with claws"), gnawing on the wooden supports in the antiques shop and upsetting every shelf, has set the stage for tourists, who, Buckminster said, observing chaos do not hesitate to upset things even more.

Buckminster set his biggest wire trap for the raccoons but caught, instead, first a cat and then a dog. The cat did not make the same mistake twice, but the dog walked into the trap three times. Three times, Buckminster released him and the dog began to adore this man who always set him free. Buckminster, who prefers cats, was irritated by the dog's poor memory, not to mention the dawning of its hapless trust.

Sometimes his stories of wildlife take on a moralizing intensity. Take the pileated woodpecker, for example, who, twenty feet up in a tree, hammered out a prodigious hole. In 1995 I had accompanied Buckminster to marvel at this cavity. When the tree blew down two years later, a limb rolled over on top of him as he was sawing it into firewood, pinning him to the ground and cracking two ribs. The bird, he said, was perhaps taking revenge for its loss. Months later, knowing the woodpecker had returned to find a puny, rotten log in place of its tree, he decided to find "something better" for it. I pictured him uprooting a huge insect-ridden tree as a gesture of appeasement, for he had entered the force field of the bird and could not escape.

Buckminster himself like a shadow moved intangibly across the land. For years now I'd seen him slip graceful as a cat in and about his property. When he wasn't in the dooryard or holed up inside, he was on a mission, often looking for a tool he "just saw somewhere." He covered several miles a day within his own domain. Wherever I went I might catch sight of him, but not see him coming. Sometimes he appeared in parts—legs dangling over the edge of a scaffold, duck-bill cap bobbing through branches, or eyeglasses at a distance, flashing code. I know he has spent decades stashing things away and ripping up the rotten roofs and yet, like a walker traveling light through the world, he gave the impression that he was just passing through, making small adjustments to the stage set as he went.

Over the years Buckminster has dragged me to inspect bushes, flowers, and nests. He has planted trees, grasses, and masses of yellow iris. He has taught abandoned red-winged blackbirds to fly. During the late summer days, with bemused wonder, he will gaze upon the silvery pampas grass rising from the water, alert in the afternoon to enhancement of its sheen by the sun.

Marshland once the ice rink, where camouflaged carp still swim, surrounds the pampas grass. The occasional volunteer alder contends with sodden roots half the year, and ice the rest. Each step around the cottage is a step into bogland. The marsh has a dark open swath of water between the grasses that, once photographed, resembled the shadow of a hulking human figure—a hockey player or a woman built like a Mexican pyramid, with a bun—a woman, as Buckminster's mother used to say, "ugly as a stump fence."[1, 2]

Ten years ago, on this site, Buckminster chopped down a hundred-and-fifty-year-old apple tree hollowed out by lightning. Over several visits I took pieces of the tree trunk home. Each time I hauled another section to the car I told Buckminster that he should come see me sometime, check out the studio, visit this tree. He said politely, "I will." All along I had collected stones and crooked sticks from Owls Head but now I realized, like many collectors before me, that I was attempting to take all of nature home. One day, although I do not and will not collect taxidermy, I asked Buckminster if, by chance, he had a seagull. Yes, but it was a gull made of bronze, he said. When I asked to see it even so, he could not oblige, saying, "Oh no, there's too much debris between me and that gull."

In time, having collected so much for "what else it is," I decided to test the verisimilitude of certain discoveries on the experts. My tendency to assign bogus chronologies and histories to artifacts was endlessly entertaining, like rearranging the rock garden had been when I was six. Was it important? I didn't know. But it was fun to find charred tankards from medieval kitchens, a toy dog on wheels as a (failed) prototype for the Trojan horse. That certain impressions in the blown-out retread tires found in ditches resemble fossils from the Permian period made me wonder who else might think so. I took a chunk of this rubber, imprinted with shapes bearing uncanny resemblances to the fins and ribs of ancient fossil fishes, to the museum at Harvard and, concealing the giveaway tread marks on the backside, asked two young paleontologists if they could identify the species of these fish. Tracing the feathery gouges they saw fish where there were none. How many? Two. Or—yes—three! Which species were they? Did they date from the Permian, age of coal, or—and this seemed more likely—from the Devonian period, famous for the explosion of fishes?

In July of 2002, Buckminster and I took a walk up through his woods on the backside of the pond.[3] We climbed up over spongy pine-needle floors, over boulders, and around uprooted trees whose undersides revealed deep clefts and roots hanging with clots of dirt and stones. The pond was now far below. Buckminster said that the Indians who had lived here chipped points out of the granite slabs and, indicating several hollows where there were smaller chunks of the rock, stained orange and dark grey, suggested that here were tools and this the evidence of an archaic community workshop. As the paleontologist will find a fossil where others do not and the astronomer a new solar system, so, even in the woods, Buckminster will find a workshop full of tools. These rocks had smooth sides as though hand hewn, but the edges most likely formed when the pieces split along natural faults. Doesn't one need flint or chert to make good points? This rock seemed too hard and granular besides.

There's nothing you could flake off from these. I was skeptical that Man-the-Toolmaker had fashioned these rocks. Buckminster was making deductions the way anthropologists do, but trained anthropologists and archaeologists also make mistakes when from a single tooth or piece of skull they reconstruct a hominid. As I am no geologist nor expert in Indian remains, and as Buckminster has roamed these woods—his playground— for three quarters of a century, I will not contest any theory he proposes while we are on it. I could see where he was headed with his theory of the arrowhead workshop, though—straight for the dreamer's corner.

We worked our way to the crest of his land and he showed me the fifty-foot-high white spruce tree he first climbed to survey his territory after Helen died. Even a person who didn't want to climb a tree would find it hard to resist this stairway to the sky. If only you could reach the lowest branch, ten feet up, from which point the limbs grew straight out, you could climb at easy footstep intervals almost to the top. To begin his annual ritual climb, Buckminster brings a ladder from home. "I go up forty-six feet," he said today, "not as high as a crow—a crow would sit on the very top." Once aloft, he has to peer through the top needles to see the water. As houses are built along the shore, the tall trees are cut down. The view is changing in Buckminster's favor. Every year he can see more of the ocean and the islands. Years ago he told me he wanted to build a house or tower on this spot, round like an inland lighthouse, with windows on all sides and a pool table at the top. He mentioned the project again today, but only after prompting.

On the way down the hill we looked under and into many trees. I inhaled the smell of rotted wood and loam and marveled at the deep pockets under roots that grew around rocks. It was a mysterious place. I was seeing something I was not meant to see and it was unexpectedly fecund too, for the earth was twitching with woodworms, mites, spiders, and beetles—a riot of biology. All around us, under every tree, was a potential cavern and life tearing through it. I couldn't decide now whether I was enhancing or shedding whatever standards I do have as a collector when I begged Buckminster to help me cut and carry long strands of roots and clots of dirt down the hill to my car, where I wrapped them gently in archival paper and placed them in on top of everything else.

On a cold morning Buckminster emerges from the house holding a plastic dish in which two dust-webbed olives reclined, one inside a short metal pipe. They were once caterpillars, now chrysalises, he has rescued from subfreezing weather and was keeping near the warm stove. Three months after he had found the larvae they are still wrapped in frail transforming shrouds. He believes they will survive, but he wants a second opinion. I give this problematic incubation a cursory once-over. Irritated by my obvious lack of interest in his experiment, Buckminster grumbles something like "yah, yah" and retreats into the house, like a child whose toy had been scorned. We are, for once, truly out of sync.[4] I wish, for Buckminster's sake, to conjure up a more sympathetic audience. I cannot import a real biologist soon enough to save these cocoons, but from the historical past I choose a man prepared to admire the minuteness of much of the *naturalia* of this place as well as to take the chaos of its *artificialia* in stride. I imagine the British collector Dr. James Petiver (1658–1716) transported from the time of William and Mary to today, Owls Head, Maine. Petiver, like Buckminster, according to contemporary accounts was all too familiar with disorder.[5]

I imagine Petiver standing in the dooryard shoulder level to Buckminster's biceps. He has a coarse and reddish face and is dressed in his London clothes of the era: scarf, ruffs, and a preposterous wig. He has brought along a pile of albums from his insect collection. In this ahistorical moment, Buckminster stands beside his confrere in faded khaki pants, windbreaker, and, concealing his billiard-bald head, his Tenants Harbor hardware store cap. At 5-foot-6, Buckminster measures a good four inches taller than his visitor and is, comparatively, a wraith, a musty twentieth-century journeyman clutching a dish of dormant olives. Petiver points distractedly to his own stack of papers wrapped around as yet unmounted butterflies. An offshore breeze blows several of the album pages out of his hands and across the yard. Buckminster puts the caterpillars on the hood of the Ford Fairlane and tries to retrieve these tattered flakes of *Danaus plexippus*, butterflies commonly called "milkweeds."

Petiver, now picking up an eviscerated toaster, extracts the small wrapped pieces of isinglass (or mica) from between the wires. He has always used sheets of mica to cover the insects before he mounts them in the albums—a technique that he himself invented. It was a good idea that this otherwise slovenly collector had, for between mica, as if trapped in eternal ice, the illusion of the insects' permanence is assured. Petiver now sorts through Buckminster's gears and wheels and wires. He has collected both natural and artificial objects from the colonies, but who knows what he thinks of this futuristic place? He might employ a strategy for understanding these man-made objects from the future in terms of the natural world. After all, as a collector of arcane artifacts from abroad, he had seen many things for the first time. In the eighteenth century, when men still believed in *God the Clockmaker*, it was not unusual to describe natural phenomena in terms of the mechanical world.[6]

As a voracious collector of botanical specimens Petiver finds insects, plants, and vines in Owls Head like the kinds he has at home. "Milkweeds?" Buckminster says, returning empty-handed (the wings of Petiver's dried butterflies have withered to his touch). "I'll show you some milkweed . . . it's a pest." He leads Petiver down to the edge of the swamp. "I thought there would be *Danainae*," Petiver says, as Buckminster waves toward the white fluff emerging from thin pods. At first he is dismayed that this man from the future did not understand that "milkweed" referred to the butterfly itself—but then, taking a second glance, he realizes he has seen *no such plant as this one* west of Bathgate. Buckminster gives him a stalk to take away and while the two are talking, a new species of *Danaus plexippus*, a large monarch butterfly, related to but, with its four-inch wingspan, far more magnificent than Petiver's *Danainae*, now in shreds, flies in from central Mexico, a little off course on its way to Canada, and lands on the milkweed. Petiver eagerly traps the butterfly with a nearby piece of fishing net, the close-woven kind, used to catch sardines. Buckminster stands by as Petiver takes a rag from his intricate pocket and smothers the monarch. "But it was about to lay its eggs!" Buckminster, defender of all living things, protests. "And the caterpillars *eat* milkweed!"

Enough of this. I go back to rooting with black fingernails into the scrap.

8

STILL POINT

It's all in the wrist with a deck or a cue,
And Frankie Machine had the touch
He had the touch, and a golden arm.
                              —Nelson Algren,
                              The Man with the Golden Arm

It's easy to conjure up a British butterfly collector remote in time; it's quite another to bring along my own contemporaries to Buckminster's because I forget how they will impinge upon my vantage point. One morning, just last year, I asked a friend as we stood mesmerized by the sight of various metals made brighter by the rain, "Isn't this beautiful?" Of course I expected her to answer yes, but instead she said, "Not many would agree with you." "I know that!" I snapped, annoyed.

Friends will not only give me a hard time, but they will compete for the very best stuff. In the beginning, I was uncertain which things *were* the best, but now, like a seasoned bird-watcher, I spy the glint and flicker of a rarity, and like a bird-watcher protecting her life list, I would rather die than *not get there first.* In the presence of competitors, I feel such atavistic impulses as coveting and pillaging coming to the fore. What if someone else were to find the equivalent of the book-nest or the fossilized typewriter and buy it from Buckminster without asking me first?

Caught off guard by the bucolic outback, at first novice visitors seem disappointed, even bored. There's nothing good here—for them. But I believe that this place, like a garden of collective memories, has the power to make people want things...even sordid things, and sure enough, as time goes by, and I witness how they work the piles, my heart sinks, for—and it never fails—each *will* uncover something of profound and often personal resonance. Their eyes narrow and their faces narrow too, and I recognize the look of avidity commingled perhaps with a memory of loss—of the old milk bottle, the plastic Uncle Sam clock: *I had forgotten this...I did not mean to let it go. I have to have it back. Oh, but it isn't just yours,* I think. *It's mine too—give that to me.* I struggle against the tide when I see a friend pick up a fractured oil lamp—green and lovely—*Roman!* I think, *That lamp is Roman...and who will ever know that now?* To write its secret history I need to own it, too. I am mortified at the depth of my distress. Who knew how Roman trash can be?

As my friends approached Buckminster to settle accounts, some argued with his prices, breaking an unspoken rule: *This is Maine, not Morocco!* One spent half an hour beating down the price of a bicycle from ten dollars to five, crowing to me afterward that she had *tricked* him. She was not invited back. Some transgressed further. "I think I'll come back later this year, rent a house, and spend a month or two," one of these traitors declared after she'd been in Owls Head for the day. When she spoke this way, I felt that a red pig had pushed me to the wall.[1]

My artist friend Marjory Wunsch was that rare companion who in 1999 had come along just for the adventure, although the first hour of her first encounter with Buckminster was far from auspicious. He did not answer when we pounded on the door. We walked around. When he finally did appear, he did not say "Oh, *there* you are" in that affable way, as he was wont to do; he suffered the introduction to Marjory and, almost as if he did not know why we were there, he retreated into his house banging the door behind him. Like raccoons, we were plaguing him.

I thought perhaps we had caught him taking a nap. Being waked from a nap is annoying. Marjory listened to this theory with sympathy but watched the door behind which Buckminster was barricaded. His bad temper was most unusual, I said, but as she had already detected an inherent sweetness behind this temper, I did not need to explain. "Does he have medical insurance?" she asked. "Who takes care of him?" And, although Buckminster was by this time almost an octogenarian, "How did his father die?" In a fire, I told her, when Buckminster was only three. I had known this for some years now, but as it was so very sad, I had been pushing the story into a dark corner. In honing my skills for digging and collecting, perhaps I had been myopic about certain aspects of Buckminster's life. I had never, for example, asked him about his health insurance.

We walked down to the swamp where, before the rain began, I wanted to take some pictures. Marjory wore a small yellow slicker she had mistaken for her own but that belonged instead, a long time ago, to one of her children. It matched the yellow smudge of the iris beside her, now at their peak. Marjory's features through the lens of the camera consisted of eyeglass frames and a smile.

When, after a while, Buckminster reemerged, he seemed his usual affable self. I took his picture too even though I saw, through the lens, a steely stare hooded by the visor of his cap. I felt something heavy swinging in the air, like a pendulum or a scythe. All the pictures I took that day came back from the lab overexposed.

History passes from father to son.[2] But Buckminster, surrounded by the detritus of industry and the ghost of a farm, lives where he has lived almost all his life—on his mother's ancestral land. The frontispiece of his family Bible, opposite an engraving of Christ restoring sight to the blind, includes in copper point the names and dates of death of four generations of his family on the paternal side: from Joseph Buckminster in 1872 up through his father, Thomas William, who in the early 1920s came to Owls Head from Stonington: "That's about thirty miles by water and one hundred and thirty by land." Thomas, a newcomer to Owls Head, died in a fire in 1925, leaving behind his family, a small boat, and almost no money at all.

Buckminster remembers sitting across the kitchen table from his father. "He needed a shave—almost as much as I need one today." And he remembers the pedal car his father bought for him, a red Model-T. As a boy in Stonington, Tom Buckminster had worked for a woman shopkeeper who taught him to drink, and it was alcohol that did him in in Owls Head, where one day, almost certainly under the influence, he stumbled into the barn of the house where he and his family then lived, just down the road from where we now sat. "He had delirium tremens, you know," Buckminster said (in case I didn't know), "and he was probably smoking too." He said that his father must have fallen asleep, setting fire to the hay, which then exploded and burned the barn to the ground.

There was no fire department in 1925 in Owls Head and the rest of the family escaped before flames reached the house, already doomed. They carried three-year-old Buckminster up the road to Aunt Susie's, where he lives today, while their neighbors salvaged what they could: doors, windows, an antique china cabinet, and a grand piano, too. He remembers these piles; for all he knows, he said, he still has some of the original pieces. He remembers going with his mother and aunt the next day to view the rubble, but says he was too young to remember now how he felt.[3]

As Marjory's and my visit progressed, Buckminster's mood improved. "When I'm feeling low, I sometimes take *nymphobar-maid*—for depression," he told me later that week on the telephone.[4] Not only did he have medical insurance, he assured us (for I asked him on the spot), he had a doctor, dentist, and lawyer as well. Settling in for a long chat, he produced his first edition of the life of Paul Revere. I sighed and moved away as he regaled Marjory with his take on Revere as social climber and deserter from the sea battle of Bagaduce against the British fleet, "where he scuttled the ships in Castine and took off on foot." Marjory, who had expected a Down East curmudgeonly account, was charmed by Buckminster's eloquence, saying later she had never known that "Paul Revere was a such a loser with good PR." She was also impressed by the delicate gate Buckminster had woven out of twigs, the dextrous shaping of firewood along the road, and the systematic order to the tools in the foundry. While she admired, too, Buckminster's single-minded devotion to the foundry, his housekeeping had left her with a powerful negative impression. "Why doesn't he call for a Dumpster? Give it all a good coat of paint?" More than once, she said, she felt on the brink of fear. She saw that he had restored—nothing. Such chaos, after all, "is anathema to the shopper's sense of discrimination." In Buckminster's defense, I told Marjory that he always had a plausible explanation for why things were the way they were.[5]

I also told her that Buckminster had tucked single lots into designated places: buoys under the shed, teapots in the attic, and pewter in the hold. He has designs on all of them—in the future—which sounded, I had to admit, just about as good as saying *never*. (I am acquainted with this kind of future; it looms like an empty pocket, prepared to accommodate the most authentic work one will ever do—guaranteed.) Just last year, I told Marjory, he cleaned off his workbench in the basement and hung a few good tools above. During the summer he kept this room a cool 45 degrees Fahrenheit. "I don't open the door for fear the heat will cause the tools to sweat and they will rust."

"You see ?" I said. "He cares." I told her that years ago I had brought a friend to Owls Head who had attempted to organize the dense confusion in one corner of the shop. I begged her to stop. Perhaps disorder *was* the order Buckminster preferred. Once I gave a plastic box to Buckminster so he could protect the choicest of his moldering postcard collection, but when I came across that box two years later there was nothing in it. The translucent emptiness amid the clutter provided a welcome relief from incident.

"Yes, but why *doesn't* he clean the place up?" Marjory asked now, when, in the shop, I tripped over plastic containers, disgorging hundreds of metal washers down a flight of stairs. I apologized to Buckminster for adding to the mess, but he merely railed against all manufacturers of cheap plastics and, by way of contrast, pointed to a stack of metal PureLac dairy milk crates inscribed with the words: WARNING. THIS CASE PROTECTED BY PINKERTON'S NATIONAL DETECTIVE AGENCY. He had a great number of these crates, which we admired. These PureLac crates were a *good* thing. How did he come by so many? "I go with a gal now and then up in Waterville," he said. "Her family ran a dairy that went out of business about 1950." The crates are so strong that he puts one or two under the end of a plank and drives his car onto the jury-rigged ramp to fix it.

But now—what was there here that *could* be set in order? Was there a hierarchy of objects or events? Does kicking a pile of plumbing downstairs measure up against the news that Buckminster had a lady friend in Waterville? Why don't we put the washers into some of the Pinkerton crates? Would this make things better than they are now? The questions seemed as feeble as corks from Zero Mostel's popgun. Or, as a friend used to ask his brother in order to end an argument, "Which is better, a window or a crow?"

I was not responsible for spilling the washers. Buckminster was not responsible for the frailty of the plastic boxes. The only nominally responsible agency must be Pinkerton—because it is an *agency* and because it has *embossed* on the sides of its property its promise to prosecute thieves.

The east coast had been under intermittent heavy rains all week, and during a downpour that eventually drove us away altogether we took refuge in the dark barn. I had hoped Marjory would find something she might like—a mirror or a garden chair—but she found nothing, confounded, as she later said, by the disparate homogeneity of the ruins. "Wonderful array of frying pans," she said politely on the first floor of the barn, as I shone a flashlight into the rafters; "terrifying chaos," she said on the drive home.

I was looking as usual for God knows what, as a low-wattage bulb cast swaying corridors of light into the rubble. It was so dim that Buckminster decided to rig up extra light. He went back to his house, fifty yards away, and from an outlet above the (unused) front door, threaded a train of extension cords through the maze of iron bedsprings and tractor parts straining the last lines over the steps to the second floor of the barn. There he attempted to plug a lamp in a metal cage into a socket attached to the frayed cord. As it didn't quite reach he returned to the house to fetch another. During his absence it began to pour. We were one board width away from the rest of the world; in some places the walls gaped and the rain blew in. At last the bulb in the cage slung up and over a ceiling beam lit up the details of wrack and ruin. There were no rocking chairs for Marjory after all, and what had appeared to be a large dead hedgehog in the gloom was revealed as yet another electrical outlet wound thick with rusty wire. Why, I wondered, had Buckminster bothered going through the storm when a flashlight might do?

"What was he thinking?" I soliloquized on the way home (for all I could think about was thunder and lightning, depressions full of water, a hookup gone wrong, sizzle and char). "If I were to ask him, *What were you thinking?* I bet he'd say, *Well, it was going to work out just fine,* or, *I wanted to bring you some light,* and never, *Of course I thought we would all fry in hell.*"

That night Marjory and I went to watch Buckminster play pool at T. Reeds in Rockland. Cone-shaded lamps glared down onto the players and the acrid green felt of the table. The music was earsplitting, but Buckminster, partially deaf, attended only to the chalk, cue stick, and the game, tonight his favorite, nine ball. His face revealed—nothing—as he executed each move. Making an arc with his stick while barely moving his lips, he would indicate to his opponent the precise trajectory he proposed each ball would take. He would then tap the cue ball with supreme delicacy, sending it off charged with momentum. It kissed the first intended designated ball and rebounded to split between the next two balls at the opposite end of the table, knocking both into predetermined and separate pockets, located nowhere near their original positions.

In between shots he would circle the table like a military strategist analyzing the maps, blue-chalking his cue before each shot. He sometimes used a bridge or made his shot with one leg stretched along the rail of the table to gain height, graceful as a lizard. He was long accustomed to winning tournaments for miles around, ending up one year in Las Vegas sponsored by Budweiser as the third-ranked player from the state of Maine. Tonight, however, a redoubtable, snaggletoothed fellow he'd been coaching for months won every game. He played with some of Buckminster's grace and owed, I thought, not a little to his mentor.

Buckminster is always the oldest contender, often by almost sixty years; for this reason alone he is an anomaly. But as his game is always elegant and his manners, too, space surrounds him as if he were playing in a different era. His own mentor, when he was fourteen, was Morris "Oskie" Johnson, railroad worker, crack hockey player, pool hall genius, and also a perfect gentleman. Buckminster follows Oskie's lessons to the letter.

For two years after the car accident, Buckminster's injuries kept him at home, but by 1997 he was back on track, chopping his "cord of wood before breakfast" and playing pool several times a week. Two nights running, in early October 2001, I went with friends to watch him play in back-to-back tournaments, the first night in a bar in Camden, the second in the country. The games progressed with winners replaying losers and losers losing more than once, but, even then not yet out of the running. The list of the players' rotation looked as complicated as a family tree. In a dim corner, behind a tall plant, Buckminster and his cue stick remained wedged between games. He nursed a king-size Pepsi. My friend was famous, a threat to all comers. "Do you know who you're looking at?" a kid asked me as Buckminster hunched to set up the balls inside the triangle. "Yes I do," I replied, cool as a stage mother. "He's the best," the kid said, "…the best," and, I think, "the still point of the turning world."[6]

No matter where his opponent was at the time (for, between turns, some did wander away from the table), if Buckminster failed to execute the move he had predicted, he would insist on relinquishing the play, even though, as he told me afterward, "Sometimes the hit is so thin, it is hard to judge." In two evenings of perhaps sixteen games, he gave up his turn twice on the grounds of such unfulfilled intentions. This ritual of honoring promises confounds his opponents, most of whom practice no such courtesy.

There was a more or less uniform raucousness in the bar in the heart of Camden, but a jungle blend of uneasy truces and swift retributions in the second, a country roadhouse outside of Belfast. The reputation of the place was revealed by the raised eyebrows of those who'd given us directions along the way. Later, I asked Buckminster to compare the clientele at the two bars. "Oh well," he said, "it's just one town and another." Here, tempers simmered. Arguments broke out like random firecrackers, and a hand-lettered sign proclaiming penalties for fighting gave testimony to previous evenings of unrest. YOU FIGHT, YOU'RE OUT—FIRST TIME THREE WEEKS—SECOND TIME THREE MONTHS.

Sometimes at home around a porch light an insect we've never seen joins the crowd of *Ordinarius*. So, too, society of the night in the roadhouse brought out some monstrous bugs. As if from distant galaxies, misshapen women entered, huge, greasy, coupled. No one in the karaoke pit sang on key, and at the bar a guy showed his bottom to us all. The dominant males took turns strutting back and forth, making theatrical entrances or exits, as if to test the limits of their autonomy, shouting abrupt profanities. You could not tell through the fragmented yips and yells just what was going down. One of Buckminster's opponents, stocky, in paint-splattered clothes, paced up and down the row of pool tables slapping each in a long string of banners advertising beer, in repetitive high fives, snarling, "Goddamn he's good. He always wins!" He could not accost Buckminster directly on account of age and venerability, but he could displace his anger with blows to the banners: *Take that, old man, take that.* Buckminster was protected by his deafness; his steadfast tactics did the rest. His natural jocularity does have a puerile quality but tonight, even as his opponent wandered off to get a beer, he continued to mouth his intended next move to the air, projecting sobriety and focus, while from the bar "Screw you, screw bin Laden" ricocheted off the walls. In general, his opponents treated him with deference, but as they came more from pinball than nine ball, that deference included a touch of bewilderment, if not out and out frustration ... *goddamn, how'd he do that?*

I had a bad dream in which two old ladies bought Buckminster's. They cleaned it up and sat out front in rocking chairs. I know what it looks like when easy living comes along. One day, at the end of August, the personification of all I feared passed back and forth in front of Buckminster's—two miniature poodles twinkling ahead of their owner, who wore plaid Bermuda shorts, and I thought, *You know, there goes the neighborhood.*

9

THE FOUNDRY

What is it like to find the Holy Grail? It is unpeaceful and uncertain . . . it is confounding too. There is an impulse to continue searching as if it hadn't happened, and find it all over again or find another. There is momentum to the routine of many, many days.
        —William Burt, *Shadowbirds, a Quest for Rails*

In 1989, when Wendy Kaminer had asked Buckminster what he was looking *for* he said, "the Holy Grail." The metalsmithing tools he had found fifty years ago, which he claims constitute "the earliest existing brass foundry in the entire country," are the focus of his passion as a collector. And although he "has always had illusions about bumping into a pewter shop" (by which he means an *antique colonial* pewter workshop), possession of this foundry is "the closest I will come to the grail."[1]

Attending a yard sale in Warren, Maine, in 1951, Buckminster saw the remains of a small building described as an early brass foundry. "I discounted the whole thing as an old wives' tale," he said. But fifteen years later, revisiting the site to attend an estate sale, he wandered into the barn where, high up, under piles of hay, he discovered tools that represented the inventory of an antique smithy's shop. He spent the afternoon diving into the hay, head first and upside down into barrels of the treasure. By the end of the day, he said, "I had swallowed approximately a ton of hay." Whatever the original owner had made with such wonderful tools, he told me, must have been "for his own amazement and amusement." Among the tools Buckminster uncovered in his scramble were a small hand-rolling mill, lathes, a coining press, sand molds, and many crucibles—everything in fact that one would need as a smith, except the furnace itself. He acquired the cache without any difficulty and after careful research established its provenance.[2] He had, he declared, discovered, rescued, and identified the contents of the brass foundry established by William Webb (1773–1865), son of a silversmith, brass smith, and coach maker originally from Boston. "Some of it got away," he said of the contents of the original press. "I kept an eye out for the rest and bought it back." As the years went by he acquired more objects made and signed by Webb: whale-oil lamps, andirons, and candlesticks. He is enthralled by information gleaned from Webb's personal journal. He has studied the design and purpose of each tool connected to Webb's enterprise but has not himself experimented with any of them. "I might be tempted to duplicate his work," he said, "and someone might end up thinking of it as an original." *He is Webb's successor*, I thought, *he's just off by two hundred years.*

One day, when for the umpteenth time I ask to see the foundry, Buckminster pries the lumber strips from the door of the captain's house, leads me through corridors of car tires, fishing nets, tool boxes, storefront signs, decoy duck heads, and sea glass by the crate, and up the stairway littered with raccoon's leavings of crumbled cork floats. The door to the foundry artifacts is tied—over and over by a loop of string from a nail to the knob. Webb's presses are set up inside—crucibles, irons, anvils, andirons—systematically laid out in categorical order on long trestle tables. A few mysterious wrapped and tied packages of materials never used remain after two centuries in their original paper.[3] High boots "belonging to the boy," Buckminster says (referring to Webb's son), stand in the middle of the floor, tied together with thick twine so that they would not, even in a high wind, be separated. Wallpaper cascades down in soft folds and nineteenth-century portraits relegated to the floor bulge under dank beaded glass. One stands in a corner as disgraced. Buckminster had thought that the man in the print was a relative of William Webb. But, to his disappointment, "It turned out to be General Neil Dow, so I took him down from where he was and threw him on the floor."[4] Everywhere, stubbornly, a scent persists: something from the sea, enormous snails in brine perhaps, flavored with untold generations of mice. Buckminster pins back the wallpaper again and again, sometimes with silver duct tape, sometimes with Scotch tape, as he wages war on the continuous fall of lath and plaster.[5]

William Webb was, according to Buckminster, a great-nephew of Benjamin Franklin, "the smartest man who ever lived." Buckminster feels sympathy for Webb; apparently his family's connection to the illustrious Franklin did nothing for his own career, while, on the other hand, Paul Revere, the well-placed social-climbing son of a silversmith, received all the important commissions in Boston. While Revere was a fine metalsmith, Buckminster says, he was also a scoundrel, appropriating the ideas of others and behaving just as he chose. Unlike William Dawes and Samuel Prescott, who made it all the way to Concord to warn that the British were coming, Revere was, in fact, captured by the enemy. And that, according to Buckminster, was his own fault, "because in the middle of his famous ride, he stopped in to see a woman." Revere is more renowned than either of his fellow riders, his ride immortalized by Longfellow's poem (1861) and his social status by Copley's portrait of him, in which, holding a silver teapot, he stares out of the frame like a defiant rebel warrior. Buckminster considers the heroic reputation imputed to Revere as a result of these tributes to be an outrage, given Revere's disgraceful behavior in 1779 at the Battle of Bagaduce.[6] During the siege on the Penobscot River by thirty-seven British ships, according to firsthand accounts, Lt. Colonel Revere disobeyed his superior's orders on more than one occasion and ended his naval career by leaving his men and ship at the height of a decisive battle. Tried by a military tribunal for desertion, Revere was acquitted, because, Buckminster claimed bitterly, of "who he was."[7]

In 1799, William Webb had to leave Boston in a hurry. Buckminster thinks he had had a fight over money, for when Webb settled in Warren, Maine, with his mother, he was "four hundred dollars in the hole." Webb became the pillar of his new community, a leader in the church, and a proponent of prohibition. In the *Annals of Warren* he is referred to as Deacon Webb.

He was the only smith in town and spent his talent according to the needs of the community—repairing guns, teakettles, and clocks. In his spare time he made new objects out of silver and brass.[8]

According to the *Annals of Warren*, on April 29, 1816

The shop of Deacon Webb took fire in the afternoon and was totally consumed. Through the smoke caused by this fire, a spot, apparently as large as a musket ball, was observed upon the disc of the declining sun, and many others were, at different times, seen during the season. These, with the coldness of the summer, threw a deep gloom over the minds of many, and strengthened the notion that the order of nature was deranged, and the source of light and heat about to fail.[9]

A meteorological explanation for the unseasonable weather came later: the volcanic eruption of the island of Tambora in Indonesia in 1815 had sent a thick cloud of dust and ash into the upper atmosphere, causing, in 1816, the famous "year without a summer" throughout the northern hemisphere.

In 1997 on a dark and rainy day, Buckminster and I decided to visit the Maine State Museum in the hopes of finding a destination for William Webb's foundry. Buckminster had asked me to contact the director and make his case for him. He wanted to know if the museum (whose mandate is to collect the industrial past of the state of Maine) would buy Webb's foundry for his asking price. Though the director had expressed muted interest in the foundry, Buckminster was pessimistic. As we made plans to visit the museum in Augusta together, he said gloomily, "They spent a million dollars hauling a sawmill all the way from Cushing...don't know what they paid for it." He has few illusions about the altruism of institutions. Convinced that museums have the money, he is fatalistic about the chances of his touching any of it. They would wait, he implied, like foxes behind the woodpile, until he was no more, then hire a van and haul away his treasure.

That day at the museum, it was as if he'd left most of himself at home. He had a bad cold and sucked on menthol drops. Away from wrack and ruin he'd lost his cruising gait. "We aren't meant to walk upright," he used to warn me, "we are designed for swinging in the trees." When he wasn't sliding about on the polished floor in his U.S. Navy dress shoes, he creaked along in a befuddled, old-guy way. As he bent in to study the reconstructed rooms, his cap was knocked off by a glass partition he did not see. "Now, this can be deceiving," he said, the third time it happened. He turned the visor of his cap front to back, prompting the director of the museum (who stayed by our side from start to finish) to suggest that the visor protected both his head and his glasses from striking the pane. I welcomed the distance the glass created between us and the scenes of nineteenth-century industry—it seemed proper. Buckminster, on the other hand, captivated by so much simulated reality, clearly wanted in. It was his field after all.

Although Buckminster has no complaints about his own work for the fish industry or at the shipyards during the war, in the museum it was clear that he had empathy for every person who, in the past centuries, had worked under unhealthy conditions. Before the dim interior of a wool-spinning room, he explained how the fine filaments of wool can get into the lungs. And when we stood in front of the Portland Stove Foundry, complete with lumps of pig iron, he spoke again of the hazards. A lot of sulfur in contamination, Buckminster informed us, went back into these lumps or *blooms*. He admired *The Lion*, a locomotive used for hauling lumber from Machias Port to Orono (displayed with the 1846 map of the route). He inspected with care a cut-work shell from an outfit that made clapboard, a portable saw for veneering, a steam-engine bailer, and a "Swing Dog"—a hook and pole for logging, invented by a Mr. Peavey. He studied a display of the evolution of axes, a full-scale model of a section of a ship from the Falkland Islands, and a reconstructed gun shop complete with a rifle used in the battle at Harpers Ferry in 1859. We passed a lawn sprinkler made sometime after 1892 and a second engine of a train—"a lot of brass on there." Buckminster, who admires good workmanship at all levels of difficulty, seemed as taken by the sprinkler as by the train. He read most of the exhibition texts aloud, and, with extra relish, *Orange Grouse Salmon Fly, tied by Ai Ballou, Winthrop. circa 1930*. He was gratified to find three oil lamps and a pair of andirons made and signed by his own William Webb. As we were here on behalf of Webb, we were relieved to see some of his work already enshrined. Buckminster, who can spot a pair of andirons or candlesticks by Webb from across a crowded room, took courage from his ability to recognize unequivocably the style of one artisan to extend this connoisseurship to the style of another, working in a different medium. Before a primitive landscape painting by Charles Jackson, he announced, "Looks just like the one I have. Mine isn't signed, but I *know* it was by him."[10]

As we entered the ethnographic, archaeological, and the natural historical part of the museum, Buckminster had less to say. We saw tools of surveyors and ochre taken from Mount Katahdin by the Red Paint people. We saw adzes and markings on slate mats that bayonets had been laid on and the sixteen-hundred-year-old shell midden of the Susquehanna Indians. We gazed at a "plummet-scraper" made from a swordfish saw, and shards of rare prehistoric brick. I coveted all the nails, the eighteenth-century window glass of the French settlers, and especially *the only bona fide Norse object in the United States, 1065–1080:* a penny. The copper kettles, arrowheads, spears, and cauterizing irons from the Champlain exploration and early Native American trade reminded me of the oxidized cups and tools from Owls Head. In this room I had an overwhelming sense of equivalence; each artifact had its descendant somewhere back at Buckminster's. It made me want to return to Owls Head then and there and tear the place apart for each visual equivalent. I had moved from a mood of vague melancholy provoked by the rooms of defunct industries to one of attentiveness to the charms of every crooked nail.

In Warren, the summer and winter of 1816 following the eruption of Tambora were very harsh because of the dust that lingered in the upper atmosphere. Relief arrived only in the late spring of 1817 when, following a few warm days, on the thirtieth of April, "the air was filled with immense flocks of the common wild pigeon, some of them more than a mile in length and succeeding each other for hours, and directing their flight to the westward."[11]

Several of these soft blue and pale orange passenger pigeons were enshrined beside the museum's natural historical diorama of a northeast coastal beach populated by beavers, otters, and an extinct blond sea mink. By the end of the nineteenth century, for food, for sport, and to gather feathers (even whole birds) for ladies' hats, hunters had decimated the entire population of passenger pigeons. Some of us have heard the story many times, but even so I read the familiar text aloud to Buckminster, who now was shuffling again—a dutiful visitor who had had enough. "Raccoons can do a lot of damage," he said suddenly, provoked by the sight of the beavers and mink. "I do like skunks," he added cheerfully. "Clears out the sinuses."

10

RAG AND BONE SHOP

THING: object, article, thing, material thing, affair,
something, artifact, gadget, etwas, quelque chose,
thingum, thingumabob, thingumadoodle, thingumadad,
thingamajig, thingumajigger, thingumaree, thingummy,
doodad, dofunny, dojigger, dojiggy, domajig, domajigger,
dohickey, dowhacky, flumadiddle, gigamaree, gimmick,
gizmo, dingus, hickey, jigger, hootmalalie, hootenanny,
whatchy, widget.

—Roget's Thesaurus

THE SAME YEAR I found the lead figures under the tire strips and realized that Buckminster was looking out for my interests, I moved into my own skylit studio on the top floor of an artists' building. Everything I brought from Owls Head, including the hollow apple tree, is in this thousand-square-foot room. There are tens of thousands of objects here, organized into boxes, drawers, trunks, and cabinets and on display in glass cases and on shelves. The studio is full, but what I have is neither "comprehensive" nor complete. It is an abridgment of an abridgment. At a flea market once, I overheard an antiques dealer I could not see proclaim in a loud voice, "No discontinued Precious Moments are available." It was as if he had said, "All the good times are gone, and even if they should come back, we will have no access to them."[1] This room is full of discontinued possessions.

I slump into a chair and wonder *What have I done?* I gaze at the heaps of mallets, hammers, cement blocks, and chains. Even lightweight objects—like paper, straw, and the roots from Buckminster's hill—seem heavy, inert lumps of ephemera. Everything—heavy and light—hangs in suspended animation as if waiting for a breeze. I collected it all with such expectations at the time and now it seems obdurate and ungenerous. *What was I thinking?*[2]

Order, classification, tasteful displays, and careful labels; isn't that what museums are all about?[3]

The patchwork of corroded copper, brass, zinc, and iron that covers a twenty-foot-long wall resonates like an accidentally beautiful display from an urban combat zone.[4] Ladders, dangling telephone receivers, and empty clocks arranged on small platforms are like slices of staging for *End Game, No Exit, Three Penny Opera*. Camouflaged against the wall lean two halves of a copper bait box with four dividers apiece, containing ruined books. One claylike piece displays the warning, DO NOT TURN DOWN THE PAGES. REPORT ANY DAMAGE TO THE LIBRARIAN. Of the fifty books in one of these bookcases only seventeen titles are even partially legible; the rest have been effaced.[5] I find this restful.

The Mystery of the 13th Floor
Jack Who Perished
Business Arithmetic
Nathan Bur
Twist
The Side of the
Hooph's Suc
Over the Top

On every side are hundreds of drawers and boxes of objects chosen one at a time. This collection is up for reinvention. The ultimate value of any single thing is based on its connection to other things. But before I get to work, each is as unpromising as a chrysalis that may not hatch.

By nonmetaphorical weight, almost 100 percent of the holdings came from Buckminster's, and by actual number almost 80 percent. The rest came from flea markets and from friends—good friends who come up with, as they describe them, "perfect things." Almost all the donations come from the natural world: rocks, roots, ashes from volcanic eruptions, small skeletons of rodents, mammals, birds, and fish, bottles of poisoned beetles, fossil lemur and bird bones from Madagascar, prehistoric axes from Australia, a carved goat skull from East Timor, a hunk of bread from a World War One prison in France, and, from parts unknown, a stuffed caiman wearing a dress.

Of course I am hoarding color and texture for the sake of "making art" as many of the artists in this building do. I take pictures, I make collages and fictional scientific displays. I do not follow the Linnaean system for classifying plants and animals but reclassify objects according to their visual, cultural, or art historical evocations, in which something quite unremarkable in fact may now seem "Etruscan," "Ionian," or "Roman."

The bounty is stacked floor to ceiling. I preside over avalanches that threaten to roll down these hand-stacked mountains. Once a year, on the weekend before Thanksgiving, the building (which contains studios of almost a hundred artists) holds an open house, and every year more than four thousand people wander in and out of these private worlds, including mine. As the collection manager, what will I show them? Perhaps some kind of museum display. I consider some of the museums that might appear in this room:

Museum of Obsolete Tools
Museum of Wires
Museum of the Croquet and Musket Ball
Museum of Natural Disasters
Museum of Ruined Landscapes
Museum of Failed Attempts
Museum of Filthy Mail
Museum of Bisected Objects
Museum of Corrosion

Some of the best storage boxes in this room are rickety, rescued just this side of loam. I use the more elegant brand-name cigar boxes for—among other things—torn papers, broken glass, volcanic ash, and sand. The names on the boxes are as collectible as their contents: *Lord Puffer, Totem, Master*

Blend, Flying Foxes, Red Dot, Romeo and Juliet, Merchant's Queen, Memento, Keystone, Two Orphans, Rockefeller, 5¢ Pippins, White Owl, Black Stone, Boite Nature, Egyptian Deity, Center Union Cut Plug.[6]

The box *Tabloid* contains "other things"—a broken photographic plate of a man in a hospital bed, a toy car with the rear axle twisted at a right angle to the front, red seashells, shotgun shells, a pencil compass and a rubber brick, a celluloid rabbit with scrofulous skin, a brass-nippled light socket, and an aluminum press plate of an Ann Landers column featuring a letter signed "Belly," from a reader who cannot help swallowing his gum.

Here is a bigger box of shoes and soles: baby shoe boot, sole of a rubber boot, heel of a very narrow shoe, burned rubber sandal with insect holes, sole of shoe marked with a cross, blackened sole full of white sand, two halves of two horse shoes with nails, doll from China with nails coming down through her feet where shoes used to be.

Here is a bottomless
almost sideless
pail
a paint can with four Jim Dine brushes
anatomical lead pipes squeezed into a head
a limbless torso
arms with stripped ends
shaft of a lantern
metallic rings threaded into fish nets
hind quarters of a copper horse
leather padded tape measure with a spider's nest inside

plumbing washer
head of a former blackbird
half a hardened rubber dog
lead weight shaped at two ends like clubs on playing
    cards
pimpled hood ornament from a Packard
four broken locks
seven pairs of reading glasses
base of an oil lamp
hitching post
shattered carved macaque
porcupine quills
silk purse bisected into wings[7]

I transcribe a constellation of objects as they are adjacent to each other on the storage shelf: behind the plaster dog with cratered face and legs eroded down to the wires is a blackened branch that turns the dog into a high-key jack-o-lope with scorched antlers.[8] Felt lining protrudes from an elliptical eyeglasses case as if from a blue-tongued skink, four terminally decrepit jackknives with frozen blades and flipper-loose covers are aligned like smelts, a soiled glove is flattened into the tail of an angelfish. A clay dish holds lead shavings from the eviscerated plumbing that look like fossil *Vermicularia* (sea tube worms), while larger, wrist-sized red-stained ovals of the same lead are like manacles for slaves, streaked with blood.

It is a relief to be the curator of a collection where maintaining perfection is not the primary mission. Things change. Become less and more complex. Fall apart. So be it. As perception is a process and material conditions mutable, I am content to watch objects morph in and out of the light.

"Hey," a friend called out on a busy street corner, "I've got a *mummified cat* for you!" and so I acquired this perfect specimen complete with whiskers, claws, and a leather collar. In the studio where I classify everything—or at least attempt to—I did not immediately know where this cat fit. Eventually I placed it on a crimson velvet board under glass. It is flawless in a vast collection of the flawed.

The other cat—a cement statuette with partially amputated limbs—is, for my purpose, more flexible. Sent by a friend from Arizona, it looks like a cheetah. It is covered with pitted holes as though carved from a single block of pumice. Sprawled, blear-eyed and scrawny, it commands several feet of real estate on the shelf. Everything placed in its vicinity seems to absorb taxonomic energy from it. As its curator I must establish its significance.

For the first variation, I meditate on the nature of *Cat*. I select the brick with impressions of paw prints and three oval volcanic stones pitted by air bubbles and shaped by the tide and place them beside this cheetah. These stones that have the same texture as the cheetah illustrate a medieval myth in which *lynx stones* were said to rain down from a celestial wild cat as frozen urine pellets. Even the archaic scientific explanation for the phenomenon of lynx stones, or *lycurium/lyncius*—that they fell as volcanic projectiles (for sulfuric fumes smell like cat piss)—helps reinforce the juxtaposition of stones and cat. Both visually and conceptually these elements belong together. I add a lightning-shaped piece of melted aluminum and a bundle of thick cables fused by a car fire. Each represents the force and compression of energy that comes coiled inside a predator. Leaning against the cheetah's back, connecting the fate of a fellow organic cat to afterlife in museum storage, is a cardboard box riddled with holes (partially consumed by paradichlorobenzene) and a seashell with a long ribbed crest like a mammal's spine.

I reconsider the stone cat. Even its painted spots are porous.[9] A piece of an accordion, a worm-bored shell, worm-eaten wood, and the piece of worm-eaten bread from World War One[10] gravitate toward the cat and, as they too are full of holes, the volcanic stones and the pierced cardboard box remain. The differences between wood and stone, bread, shell, and cat melt away because they are now together as *Things that have Holes*.

A collection of holes is pure and simple. But, I then ask myself, as the curator of *things with holes*, will I now have to write some didactic text to justify the reasons for grouping these disparate objects together as well as to lecture on the value of *information that is not there*? Isn't it enough to take pleasure in the *absence* of matter? It would be, I suppose, if the holes were defined only as subtractions of substance, but they are—too bad for love of absence—much more.

Not only does the circumference, contour, depth, and shape of each hole have an independent character, but each material has its type of hole. And as the indentations in the bread are vertical holes, in the shell horizontal tracks, and in the rock uneven pits, each type of hole may be reclassified as distinct, a phenomenon that threatens to fragment the collection once again into wood, bread, and rock.

The cat, the accordion, the prisoner's bread—all have holes. I say "hole" over and over again and it whips the air, as if I were whirring a prayer wheel or a lariat round and around—*hole–hole–whole–hole*. The word ripples outward until it becomes sound without meaning. And as the meaning of the word *hole* becomes detached from its sound, it floats—*holey–holy–holi*.

The word, divested, becomes a mantra. The cheetah looks drugged and smoky like an animal god in a shrine from an ancient Indus River cult.[II] The volcanic stones now become the male principle, or *lingam*, sacred symbol in the worship of the Hindu god Shiva. So here's a third taxonomy for the cat. I add a much creased foil packet of *Langues du Chat* ("cat tongue") cookies and my own handprint of pink chalk pressed onto a piece of slate to commemorate the historical handprints one sees on the walls in the city of Agra, prints made by widows on their way to obligatory *sati* on their husbands' funeral pyres. *Holey, holy*—the meaning of the word shifts with the handprint from hollows to hallowed, to *holi*, the name both of the festival of fertility in honor of the playboy god, Krishna, staged in central India in the spring, and of the magenta dye that the celebrants throw at one another, staining the whole town pink. The chalk handprint now looks as if a dye-drenched celebrant had accidentally touched a wall. Behind the cat's head I place an unbroken golden disk. Originally a piece of a gear from a Down East fishing boat, it looks like the sun, symbol of Krishna, in Indian miniature paintings—Krishna, in whose honor perhaps this obscure shrine was built. The words *hole, holey, holy, holi* become the flypaper; having attracted objects to their surfaces by virtue of sound, they hold them together by virtue of structure.

When photographing in natural history collections I have had many a discussion with curatorial personnel about the sanctity of science and the silliness of art. A single-tooth mastodon tooth, for example, has eight pinnacled cusps; I photographed such a tooth in which the cotton became a storm-clouded sky, the cusps mountain peaks. "Look!" I said to the curator, handing him the picture. "A mountain range!" He gave it back. "It's a tooth," he said. The scientist may always need to know what something *is* but I intend to show these things, in the words of the late Minor White, photographer and pundit, *for what else they are.*[12]

Recently I asked a friendly curator why, some fifteen years earlier, he had refused to let me photograph one of his most splendid toads, crying as he did so, "Not my Booby!" and clutching the jar in his arms. Because it was a *type specimen*, he said, the most perfect carrier of the most average characteristics of its kind—characteristics by which all other toads shall be judged; of such intrinsic scientific value, he explained, that "an artistic take is not worthy of it." Although I never use artificial lights for this work, he worried that photography, pure and simple, might actively harm the toad. He thought I might "use a lens or a camera that would cause the toad to blanch." He said he *knew* that the toad would not change before the lens, but still he worried that it might. Perhaps a picture of the toad would reveal something else, unwelcome, irrelevant. After all, the photo of the mastodon tooth looked like the Andes to me and the curator of the tooth was not amused. Metaphors, to some, are like evil weeds.[13]

There is a price to pay for trusting in appearances. I have arranged eight shelves of white and green objects as though they were priceless antiques. They are worn, oxidized, with recessive layers of greens, blues, and greys. Each object is set apart in its own space and braced or cradled by a Plexiglas or wooden stand, conveying art historical provenance and value: the Ming inkstand, the bronze from ancient Athens, the adze from Down Under. Every year, visitors to the studio want to buy these priceless marvels, which are not for sale. One year I almost sold a flattened tin box to a visitor for an enormous sum of money but, in the end, held off.[14]

There is a lot of slippage between finding an object and the reinvention of it. I had faith, if not in the specific mythologies and inflated values I was creating, then at least in the spirit of it all, so that, one day, when I noticed that a particularly encrusted flashlight was no longer on the shelf, I truly believed that it had been stolen, perhaps by a jealous visitor. If only I had left the flashlight at Owls Head—to be recycled as one-dollar-a-pound scrap or to disintegrate in peace—I would not have felt the burden of its existence or, now, of its loss. The week the flashlight disappeared, I thought about insurance, storage, security, and the wisdom of ever letting strangers into the room to see this priceless collection.[15]

In the fall when the light is low, I wonder what kind of scene would best pay homage to the stripped-down economy of a life in which a few objects gathered together seem...essential. Every year, I comb the storage shelves, paring away from what one has, back to only what one might need. This divestment never succeeds. I throw almost nothing out; I never know when I might use it. I choose the perfect chair, a bentwood side chair, grey with green nails around the rim where a woven seat used to be. One warped leg rises, as if to walk away. I choose the perfect table. Its legs have rotted unevenly and its top is disintegrating into sand punctuated by protruding nails. I select a gesticulating fork and a spoon like a flat green lagoon. I find a cracked chalice Buckminster made and fill it with mussel shells. The sheer sentimentality of setting a humble table for a phantom diner very nearly prevents me from completing it.

IN THE TRENCHES

O lion, mournful Image
of Kings, sadly brought down
You are born now only in cages
In Hamburg, among the Germans.

> —Guillaume Apollinaire,
> *The Sea and the Honeycomb,*
> translated by Robert Bly

THERE ARE MANY distractions in the studio. In the green arm-chair, I sit like a sated toad taking in the world around me, but when I am working, my progress through the room is often crab-wise; my attention slips sideways on independent legs. The sun comes out and a small tin boy glows for the camera. I lose the lens cap. I find six feathers and a piece of tar, a bird hip bone shaped like the face of warty crone, but until I find the glue and the decapitated Victorian blue jay, the crone will have no body. I remember seeing a man with little more than a head; I watched as he was wheeled on a cart into the Smith-sonian museum by two women in flowered dresses. I take out my notebook to write this memory down. Then, because I happen to be writing, I make a list of everything in the box that held the hip-bone bird head. The sun shifts, I put down the notebook and go for the camera. I find the cable release, lose my glasses. Sometimes I gaze out the window, east to the Bunker Hill Monument, west to the treetops at Harvard University. Sometimes I fight my way back into sustained concentrated work as though, almost by chance, I've found the rift in the curtain that allows me backstage. I am fortunate to occupy these nested private rooms—inner thoughts and studio space; I am the boss in both places. I may sleep here, shout, dance on the table, or do nothing at all. I may do *just as I please* but that doesn't mean—like Owls Head—that this room is an easy place to be.

I placed a pocket watch and wires inside a birdhouse and on the front pasted a cut-out shape of man from an early-twentieth-century medical journal printed at a time when all private parts were, by law, concealed. The figures in this book—if necessary—wear sarongs-cum-bandages as underwear. On the women this looks like modesty. But the men have been branded. One man's bare bottom, blackened by the censor, looks burned. I pasted a group of men daisy-chained together with blacked-out genitals—fried men, like heretics, burned for blasphemy. I attached souvenirs to newspapers and aerial reconnaissance photographs of World War One bombings.[1] I used a pocket watch without hands, torn fabric as if from a biplane, a filthy playing card—the two of spades, the spades echoing the bombs in the picture. I made these memorials to commemorate the downed pilots of the war who, according to author Paul Fussell, were often found after death with singular personal amulets on or about their bodies.[2, 3]

I move in and out of this work to eat lunch and look out the window to the train tracks. Two miles away, at Harvard, the view from the fifth floor of the museum is unremarkable but the intellectual air heavy indeed. From the fifth floor here once I heard the sound of gunfire—a genuine shoot-out on the train tracks below; the escapee went back to jail. This studio is adjacent to the "real" world. On another occasion here, I saw a policeman in his car holding a large machete—"He took it off of a homicidal maniac," the building manager told me, reassuringly. One day, as I was counting the cars on the train that snaked through the industrial wasteland, a helicopter swung low and hovered just outside the window as though looking for a place to land. On the radio that evening I heard that, ten minutes after it had buzzed the building, having ripped off the roof of the MIT boathouse, the helicopter did, weirdly and terribly, crash. Most of the time disastrous events, wrecks, gun battles, bombs make huge amounts of noise. And most of the time, I hear that noise played back on the evening news. I am punch-drunk with playbacks. Once I dreamed that a dog—a medieval breed of greyhound running along a cliff—slipped and fell to its death without a sound. I didn't stay for the playback.

I have hung an empty window frame underneath a sky-light. It represents visual access out to the world or inward to this private room. I made twenty large souvenir museum war scenes out of the essences from Owls Head, using window glass—like reverse glass painting—as the supporting surface.

Each pane contains landscapes of grand country estates or museums and landscapes in upheaval from diasporas and war. Monkeys, apes, soldiers, pilgrims, and other travelers appear in blasted scenes, passing in and out of ruined buildings. Among these are armies on the march, refugees dispossessed, and primates, often in evolutionary lock-step, in transition.[4]

As if I've ever known a war. At the end of the Korean War I was eleven. I remember wanting to be the first to tell anyone who didn't yet know that *war was over.* I worked myself into a breathless certitude that now there was nothing left to fear. Incomplete or narrow perception is not necessarily invalid. I knew just enough about Lyndon Johnson's cabinet and about U.S. foreign policy to be appalled. In the late 1960s, I had the temerity to argue face to face–*get out of Vietnam*–with a powerful, near *numero uno* government official during cocktail hour with my parents. That gentleman responded with the predictable contempt expressed by the academic crowd from those Kennedy-Johnson years, "What do *you people* know? You know nothing." Okay, but I know the crack of a whip when I hear it and so said nothing, lacking both the facts and the nerve to persist. The gentleman, now in his eighties, has since written a definitive book on the Johnson years in which he includes a recanting and contrition in hindsight by himself and his fellow policy makers for the war in Vietnam. Adults who "know best" will sometimes revisit collective memories in order to repair them, "go back and fix what has been broken."[5] I thought of calling the collection of constructed war windows *You People.* That takes care of most of us, I think, and the rest of mankind too, but for the sake of the longer history, all other primates–

spider monkey, mangabey, macaque, or great ape—slipped in seamlessly beside the men.[6]

On the car radio I heard a playback of the shots fired in the assassination of Egyptian president Anwar Sadat, itself an on-air event. Things shatter like this for all of us, on a daily basis, but that day I was moved to consider the mess. I spent the next week constructing a memorial window. I ran over metal scraps with the car, broke glass already broken, scratched on wood and film with chalk, ink, and dye and on crumpled pictures of a carousel, on portraits of faces twisted in despair, museum monkeys screaming. Incorporated behind the glass is a rope tied in a noose, a piece of charred sheet, a sleigh bell like an iron mask, and a crumpled Associated Press portrait of Sadat shouting to the crowd seconds before he was shot.

Assembled by instinct, the six-paneled ode to Sadat is composed, I am quite certain, of nothing his family would recognize or condone. I go again into the war-torn mode, slapping muck onto grimy panes set in rotten casements. I think of our own assassinated leaders—JFK, Robert Kennedy, Martin Luther King, Jr. I do not claim to be next of kin. I suffer only as a member of the tribe.

World War One chose me; it lured me with its scenes of trench warfare and the dinosaur tanks, spidery biplanes and fishy dirigibles. It tempted me with ratty, ruined rotogravures from Buckminster's and it kept me in its thrall with writings by Siegfried Sassoon, Robert Graves, and Paul Fussell. It was a war-window war if ever there was one—WWI with its no-man's-land and makeshift transport systems, hero animals, including donkeys and birds, men living below the surface of the ground, changing guard at dusk and dawn, killing *entre chien et loup*, ten thousand dead in an afternoon. Rich in mud and metal, 1914–18 in the brown newspapers *does* look like a war "to end them all," strung between the Middle Ages and Marconi. Past the blur of camera movement in the battlefield shots, past the dot patterns of the page, I go straight to the faces of the soldiers. Every man has a different face, every man had a mother, and every man was *there*.

The opposite of a louse-filled trench is a fine four-poster bed where one can eat bread and honey and count the flowers in the thick carpets. Once, in Leiden, I photographed a collection of skinned dog heads, dating from the war years of the 1940s. The dogs themselves had been eaten by the starving Dutch. Later I dreamed that I slept in a regal bedroom where the carpet was composed of their muzzles. No matter how one works to cultivate privilege and luxury, the dogs of war will find you.[7]

We are in the trenches somewhere, all the time, as far as I can make out. However apocalyptic these war scenes, their density owes everything to Owls Head. As a typewriter may also be a fossil echinoid, so piano wire is the horizon off the French coast and a piece of stained lace a bloody stretch of road. One thing becomes another, the shafts of a bird feather a broken Romanesque arch, sewing threads tangled military scrap, and an ape hanging in a museum window becomes the victim of a lynching hanging from a tree.[8]

12

A WONDERFUL LIFE

In ordinary English a random event is one without order, predictability, or pattern. The word connotes disaggregation, falling apart, formless anarchy, and fear. Yet, ironically, the scientific sense of random conveys a precisely opposite set of associations.

—Stephen Jay Gould, "Betting on Chance and No Fair Peeking," *Eight Little Piggies*

IT WAS ONE OF the half dozen or so clean spring days in Cambridge—the first of May 2000—when Buckminster and I visited the Museum of Comparative Zoology together. The lawn was slathered with thick green fertilizer that looked like the brushed-on vegetation seen in museum dioramas, as though the art of model making had been extended from the exhibits department out onto the lawn. Buckminster and I had switched places—I the native by birth in a town of transients, and he the day-tripper from Vacationland. He had come by plane from Rockland that morning and he would go home that night. I had brought him to the museum where, for almost twenty years,

I had been photographing gorillas, butterflies, and fossils. Important birds are here: George Washington's pheasants, extinct great auks, and a woodpecker from the Lewis and Clark expedition. I pointed out the window grilles interwoven with feathers from the pigeons that nestle between the spikes designed to keep them away. I have wondered if these birds have any clue that they frequent the edges of what is—for their kind—a vast mausoleum.[1] The waft of chemical preservation leaked well outside the walls—the scent of mothballs drifting down, old bone smells seeping from the vents.

I left Buckminster hunched outside the building for five minutes in order to retrieve a notebook from the car. I had pointed to a spot farther down the path and closer to the entrance where we could meet, but he stayed stock-still like a mechanical figure run down precisely where I'd left him. This was the man who in Owls Head rarely stops moving unless he's on a Mountain Dew break, pointing out a bumblebee or chewing the fat. I had never seen him stand so still and bent. As it happened, he stood between the research laboratories and the museum and directly below the cross-wired office window of the illustrious paleontologist, and my collaborator, Dr. Stephen Jay Gould. He did not know, of course, whose window he might, if he turned around and stood on tiptoe, peer into. There he was, one of my icons in close proximity to another—two men whose lives are, on every level, worlds apart. Inside and just above Buckminster's head, as we were about to discover, Gould sat bathed in the glare of movie lights as he lectured to a Canadian camera crew on, among other conchological events, the importance of tracing the evolution of bivalves in one locality over many millions of years. Outside, the light was softer, a painter's light, and Buck-minster's humped back turned his jacket into a sand dune.

What does Buckminster know about bivalves? Well, for one thing, he has spent almost four score years consuming mussels and clams and at least two high school summers paving over country roads. One of these roads was composed almost entirely of shells discarded by his neighbors and their forefathers after dinner. He spent another summer relocating small ocean clams, "planting them like potatoes" in the estuary of the Monadnock River from Scarborough to Waldoboro. Dr. Gould, an expert on land snails, had spent many seasons plucking them from Baha-mian bushes and chipping them out of ancient rocks. That which Gould would dig from the ground, Buckminster was paid to cover with tar or replant in silt. Delivering fish one day in Union, Maine, Buckminster noticed rocks "inpermed with sea-shells" on the customer's porch. The stones came, he was told, from a gravel pit above the house, a pit, he estimated, "already five hundred feet above sea level." He knew (and told me I knew too) that the fossil shells appeared in these rocks because "the whole thing had turned upside down...which I think will happen again before too long."

Buckminster stayed in Boston for almost twelve hours, tak-ing an evening flight at 8:30. All day, into the evening, he con-tinued to stand still wherever he'd been left: outside Gould's window, in our dining room, on the porch. I began to feel like Simon in "Simon Says." Impulsively I took him by Gould's office hoping that the cameras had gone and that they might shake hands—shaley nails against a soft academic palm—but, from the corridor inching forward, I in pink sneakers and

Buckminster in his Navy dress shoes that squeaked, realized as we approached the floodlit room that this introduction was not to be. As the flavor of a media event spilled out in a tangle of wires and lamps onto the linoleum floor before us, I drew back and took Buckminster with me, two mice skittering away from Gould's great voice spouting forth hypotheses with his singular panache. I am not certain Buckminster knew why we were at first tiptoeing forward and then running away; he simply followed the lead in an alien land and asked no questions. "He's one of a kind and so are you," I'd say should he ever ask why I wanted him to meet Stephen Gould. So why did we run away?

Come to think of it, I have had practice retreating from the dens of great thinkers all my childhood and, perhaps less becomingly, into middle age. In grade school, high school, even in college I sneaked past my father's study door in order to escape; I was almost constantly in academic trouble and my father took it upon his busy person to tutor, instruct, and cajole me, as he put it, into "settling down." In response to the restrictions placed on my mobility, I was, almost always, as they say, *out of there*—out the front door, out the back door, over the porch rail, and, from several rented summer houses, out the bedroom window onto the roof and down to the ground almost every night, away to the beach. To this day, I see no summer house without planning an escape route. When I stare at important books, fondle, covet, even collect them, part of me wants to *get it over with*: get out of the house, find my friends.

But here we are, Buckminster and I, at Harvard University! And of course we must profit from our proximity to greatness.

Once inside the museum, Buckminster is a perfect visitor. We see the butterfly display, the glass flowers, and the minerals from New England mines. He stands absorbed before early photographs of miners from the quarries in Thomaston and Vinalhaven. He seems to blend into these photographs—grey men against grey rocks. He moves from case to case, acknowledging every lump of ore or quartzite and reading each description aloud. I feel discouraged. I have been here so many times and remember not one rock.

Almost every weekend our parents planned trips to museums and I have been coming to this particular one since the age of three. I associate it not so much with rocks and minerals (although it has world-class collections of both) as with plaster-cracking giraffes and apes with painted gums and real fangs. As a child, I felt a kind of low-grade terror as we moved through room after room, floor to ceiling of antelopes, pangolins, gorillas, and bears crammed without adornment behind glass.

"What if all the animals came to life at once?" one of our sons, at age four, asked when I took him—the next generation fated to be spooked—to the MCZ. There would be lots of straw and splintered wood and glass on the floor, I told him, quite a mess, but I knew that he had recognized the animus no preparator's work could eradicate. No matter how many artificial parts went into simulation, the real animals were *still there*. At the moment my son asked the question, I thought I saw out of the corner of my eye a hairline tremor that might precede the communal force of wild things trampling through the glass.

After Buckminster has made a full circuit of the history of mining in New England, I lead him through the two taxonomic arrangements of the animal kingdom (by geography and by species), past the Bengal tiger and the murky room of deep-sea fishes toward a display I most particularly wanted to him to see— the model of a Pacific atoll. As serene as the surface of a pool table, this painted plaster model, a bird's-eye view of coral reefs and curling foam, is set in shallow blue-green seas. Tiny ships on steel pins inserted at varying heights around the curved perimeter simulate perspective at the horizon. We try the closed door to the room of the atoll but it has a CODE-ONLY STAFF-ONLY keypad, and we cannot get in.

One of the few times I flew rather than drove to Rockland, the plane passed over the ghostly spires of the Dragon Cement plant. The ground and quarries were dusty white under a per-manent haze of blasted rock, but pools of water like corroded Roman coins flashed up as dark a green as the deepest water around the atolls.

Buckminster had taken a plane today for the third or fourth time in his life. He had sidled into the terminal under the watch-ful eye of a fellow passenger, a man about the same age, from Vinalhaven. "You going to be all right now?" he asked Buckmin-ster, who seemed dazed. "I *think* so—oh there you are!" Buck-minster responded, catching sight of me, and looking more alert. "Almost left my wallet at the airport." His new pal was hovering, not quite ready to release him into the hands of a stranger without first giving a report. "He seemed confused," he told me, "almost missed the plane." I thanked him for watch-ing over the infrequent traveler, as one thanks a courier for the transportation of a rare art object. Buckminster, limping, followed me through the airport, keeping pace like a shadow, a good child by my side. He sat quiet as we negotiated the Boston traffic and, while he did not know what would happen next, he was calm and not afraid. I, on the other hand, was on high alert, the way one is with a passenger who may at any moment forget where he is and open the car door onto the on-ramp of a highway. After all, I carried precious cargo.

I also knew that by taking Buckminster to the studio I was inviting him to inspect again his foundlings. Would he insist on taking them back?

I needn't have worried. Even as he crosses the threshold of the studio, he is saying that it is amazing... *absolutely amazing.* I lead him over to the long metal wall, where the bookcases lean, show him the storage shelves, the green and white objects and the table where I have composed small things as though each was a syllable or a word in a line of poetry. He relaxes, and although he recognizes many of his former wares, he exhibits possessiveness toward none of them. He does not behave as I do when I visit him, wandering and distracted, my desire for certain things masked as civil curiosity. He admires the contents of the room as though he has never seen anything like it before. "The garden club ought to see this," he says, and then, acknowledging the profound relationship between his place and mine, "I don't suppose they'd appreciate it... it wouldn't matter whether it was here or in my yard."

We stay in the studio for several hours. He sits facing the metal landscape wall in the green vinyl armchair that belonged to my father. I take black-and-white photographs of him against the scrap metal, which, when the film is developed, looks like a receding series of planes and valleys. I am not too happy with

the effect of Buckminster's clothing through the viewfinder—
it is a hybrid, dingy costume. He is wearing a tan hat and padded
light blue jacket with decorative stitching over the pockets like
a child's snowsuit. He is wearing his usual chinos with the
enlisted man's spit-shined shoes. But I am so happy to see him
here. Would he mind? Standing here? There? "Set me up anywhere," he says.

TRANSCRIPTION

Their squirrels are much bigger, they call them macaques.
   —local Bhutanese guide speaking of wildlife in India

TRANSCRIBED FROM a recording made on May 1, 2001, the day
Buckminster visited the studio.[1]

B: *This I recognize—*
R: It's a beauty.
Look at the grain—mmmm.
Beautiful, beautiful chair. I made this display as if—
Hmmm . . .
—ah—archaeology—
Hmmmm.
—dusty too.
Hm.
That—must be . . . ?
I'm not sure about that.
. . . makes it not quite all yours—here.
Ah but the most of it is—

Oh yes. And these–these came from the rungs of the chain over
    there–

Ah.

These are the links ...

I see.

These are the links that–broke out ...

Corroded.

Exactly.

Yup.

R: What is this?

B: *Aluminum clipped around another piece of aluminum or cop-
    per wire, one or the other just to–see, this would be one wire
    and this would be another wire and they had a tool to clamp
    it together.*

And this?

*This is an electrical connection, and that, electrical wire, and that
    has somepin' to do with electric.*

Part of a hanging lamp ... not sure.

This?

This here.

Oh. It might be a–

Isn't there a chain around it? Or was. I think it might have been.

Of a hanging lamp?

Part of–

Oh no, it's a gas–it's a cap ... goes on some kind of tank, see what
    I mean?

Oh "full," okay–think you're right.

And this a part of a Bernzomatic torch–
What's that?
A flame spreader... instead of the flame coming out round–
–Spreads it.
Spreads it.

B: *That was in a fire.*
R: Nails stuck–
I had a lot of stuff from the Samoset Hotel.
You still have some?
Might have one or two pieces around...
I have a big hunk of it.

B: *What's that... huh, this, that, this, hold on–*
R: A great percentage–comes from your place.
Yup. This hood ornament.
Yes, everything. This table, this folding table.
Yup, sewing table.
Haven't used that recently.
You haven't used it?
Not recently, no.
[laughs]
I will.

B: *I don't recognize that.*
R: That's from a long, long time ago,

Wait–

A long time ago.

I recognize the design.

Yup.

But not the shape . . . probably a gas tank on a boat.

This weather house comes from you.

Oh.

Hansel and Gretel. Hat, hat block.

To block hats–from the pool room corner of Park and Main–

Oh yeah.

–just as you're comin' in.

Oh yeah, what's it called?

Reeds, T. Reeds.

Hmmm.

But this little guy came from Albania–

Funny ball.

–old golf balls–some quite valuable.

Do you remember the horse?

Yes!

Remember where you had it?

Down back . . .

On a pedestal.

Yah.

Because he was set up, I didn't think he was for sale.

I see [laughs].

B: *Where'd I pick that up? There?*

R: Oh, anywhere.

That is a beautiful piece of wood.

Another by the kitchen and one at home too.

Seine floats . . .

Seine?

Seine floats, for catching herring. Lead weights. Took the nets down to circle herring–they couldn't get out.

How do you spell it–*seine?*

S-e-i-n-e I think, that's right.

Seine floats.

Nice, very, Seine floats. They hand turn 'em–all different.

Up the corner–

Came out of an old Easy washer.

Came out of a–

–big copper tub–

Never got a round one from you.

B: *I don't remember but I remember this, though–*

R: –yeah–

–roller skate.

If you see anything you want back . . .

No, no.

Is it–what you told me–arbor vitae?

Lignum vitae.

Lignum vitae. Oh, it's stuck on there–

A very . . . heavy wood. Matter of fact it doesn't float. Maybe dragged up by a scallop fisherman.

Why was it in the water to begin with if it doesn't float?

The ship probably sank.

R: Is there any way we can get this off–

B: *You hold . . . no, just get out of my way–*

–all right, okay–trying to take lignum vitae off . . . off a . . . off a . . . thank you. Look at the face!

Yah.

Nice!

It was–

–beautiful!

–a small sailboat, something like a Friendship sloop or something of the sort. It's the heaviest wood.

Amazing.

Used to support shafts.

R: Nice bricks.

B: *This–ah–this . . .*

I wanted the other one but it was gone.

Ice-cream parlor. Wasn't there another one?

I looked–there wasn't–but maybe you moved it

–maybe got moved . . .

Yeah.

Saw one of the covers.

Oh!

Other day I took that birch tree down.

Right.

It was–

R: Do you recognize this?

B: *I do, I guess.*

Comes from that old dump...

Oh yah, the dump!

You know the ash, shell, pinecones...

Used to eat a lot of clams, everybody did.

When we–

In fact the street below me was more or less paved with clamshells.

Handle's bent–

This I recognize. I used that–

You did?

It's probably zinc in there–this frypan. I was casting a zinc mold.
To get it into the stove and I poured it out of here... This
here came from the Samoset Hotel–

Right.

It burned, the hippies burned it–

No–

Supposedly. They did.

Right. Right. Good excuse. That's a lot of plumbing, isn't it?

Bought nearly two ton of it. These are all codfish–

Weights–

–sinkers. They'd make soundin' leads, recessed in here and they'd
drop down them to tell how deep the water was, but they'd
also pick up parts of the bottom of the ocean so they could tell
what it was like down there–whether it was sand or clay–

So detectors...

R: You know these rings for early lobster pots?

B: *Right, right.*

Made by softening the stick over a fire—

Yeah.

And then binding it together, is that right?

I don't know, they might have, ah—

—or just bent supple sticks—

Yeah.

And tied the ends together.

They're black . . . they tarred them.

Tarred them? That's why I thought, a fire.

*Now they might have. They might have used a little steam to
    soften it.*

Yeah. But what's the stuff that ties it?

That's twine.

Old, old twine.

Old, old twine.

How old are these?

*Go back to 1900 anyway—from the time they first made traps we'll
    say. At one time they didn't think lobsters were eatable.*

I wonder when the first lobster was eaten.

Must—

—sure—

. . . have been by mistake.

Probably a drunk.

Right . . . someone quite drunk I'd say. I got—

Let's get some water—

I got a little—

—and see if we can—

*I got a little drunk one night and goin' down to the pond I got some
    frogs' eggs–*

—sit down. I have to sit if I hear this story.

I called Poison Control before I ate 'em so I wasn't that drunk.

You got frogs' eggs out?

What's that?

Frogs' eggs?

*I don't know whether they were frogs' eggs or toads' eggs, but they…
    I thought they would fry up like fish roe.*

You called Poison Control before you ate them?

*Yes I did. I tasted them but it wasn't anything I wanted … a gooey
    mess.*

So who did eat the first lobster?

I'd say the first lobster, the guy was drunk.

Yah, but if he was drunk, who was going to believe him?

And what about the second guy?

14

THE BARN

I look at the natural geological record, as a history of the
world imperfectly kept, and written in a changing dialect;
of this history we possess the last volume alone, relating
only to two or three countries. Of this volume, only here
and there a short chapter has been preserved; and of each
page, only here and there a few lines. Each word of the
slowly-changing language, in which the history is
supposed to be written, being more or less different in the
interrupted succession of chapters, may represent the
apparently abruptly changed forms of life, entombed in
our consecutive, but widely separated formations.
    —Charles Darwin, *On the Origin of Species*

ANYONE, I SUPPOSE, who contemplates desiccated animals and altered objects for a living is bound by one box or another: camera, cabinet, room, or institution within which floats the dark box that is the imagination. I am stuck with containment. And yet I am always trying to pick the lock. Over the years at Owls Head I have found chests of hide or leather and tool kits rusted shut, some full, others decayed, the contents long gone. Sometimes when I lift a box, the bottom falls out and I'm left holding the frame. Sometimes I pull what seems like an intact chest from the ground, only to find that the sides have dissolved into soil walls imprinted with worm tracks or indentations left by nails and screws. Solid boxes, shadow boxes; the heft of one reveals the other but sometimes they are glued together—shadow and substance—and I struggle to pry them apart.

Of all the boxes here, the three-story barn is the biggest. Its walls are cracking and its insides spilling out. It contains so much that it would take years to transcribe the contents but there are always piles of history from which the visitor may pull episodic threads.

The shingles that cover the barn droop in folds, crunch into the corners, and splay across the broad sides, as if, when no one was watching, the building had attempted to pull away from its foundations like an immense animal. There are two ways in. On the south side, Buckminster moves the two-by-fours that hold a hingeless door in place. It floats for seconds, until he shifts it two feet down to the granite ledge that serves as the front step. The door on the east side is an airy hole in the wall, eight feet in diameter, covered by a bright blue tarpaulin. The tarp, shredding in slow motion over the years, has become a veil of fibers—a faded sky-blue fishnet entangled in the vines and trees. Beneath the tarp is a makeshift barrier of plywood strips. This has presented no obstacle for animals wanting in. I, too, squeeze in between the slats. Once inside, a mound topped by wads of limp papers and books rises from the threshold, forcing me to stagger against the outer wall, body tight against the wood, one foot in front of the other. It is like walking along the inside of the first stage of an armature built by a taxidermist in the re-creation of a colossal animal.

The last time cows and horses lived in the barn was seventy years ago, but the place is never free from the creaking, sighing rustle of smaller animals at work. I hear sounds from wind, rain, rodents, and the subtle shifting of a load as it settles farther into the ground. I feel the subterranean tremors as a lingering reverberation like a long musical note or as the groaning of that large animal trying to walk away.[1]

Inside this building, a force much larger than Buckminster's red pig seems to have come up from underneath and exploded through the dirt floor; local history has breached the surface. Order and the earth have ruptured, and archaeology, indigenous, imported, and extending back two hundred years—along with biological remains in various stages of corruption—have worked themselves down or back up through the ground. Churned over and over as Buckminster added new loads (a process that had more or less stopped by the mid-1980s), the piles were violated by avid pickers who, in massive raids ten years later, wallowed through the superabundance of each of the three floors, rooting, penetrating, tossing the staggered piles. And because it is easy to believe one has found an antique when working in the dark, the pickers' goings-on included wholesale tossing of whatever seemed tempting outside the barn, where many objects, rejected in the end, now rot like burst fruit under the open sky.

Decay is rarely tasteful. Unlike the metallic hills outside, the mountain behind the tarpaulin is no edifice of salt-kissed scrap metal but a great greasy outcropping of law books, yearbooks, pocketbooks, Chinese lanterns, and mousetraps—objects from the world of learning, spending, celebrating, capturing. There is no space between the mousetrap and the statute of limitations. Hanging from the rafters are nets, the blades of antique ice skates, railroad lanterns, iron skillets, and, against the walls, tree hooks, long saws, and a carved hay rake with curving tines. The geometry of the building rarely achieves a right angle—the swollen beams, the swaybacked staircase, the broken foundations form approximate triangles, rough rhomboids, and a number of parallelograms where hand-cut boards have slid across each other like plates along a transverse fault.

When I first explored the barn in the early nineties, a beam had fallen slantwise to block the way. I crawled over, I crawled under. Crawling under, while easier, brought me into tight proximity with the always sodden floor, a mixture of mud and fust and mold, shallow in places like a partially exhumed grave in which clothes and paper, tinsel, ribbons, and children's games were united at random. I kicked back a cloud with every step; I climbed over ironing boards, mirrors, picture frames, crutches, chairs, and, although I never stepped on one, upon occasion I would catch a whiff of a decomposing animal. The place was leaky, it was porous, intruders dropped in through the roof or wriggled up from the floor. Once I saw a red fox streaking from underneath the building and I wondered what else sleeps, breeds, and dies in here.

What this barn needs is surely not more philosophy but a backhoe and a wrecking ball.[2] However, just when I thought I'd seen it all, some hint that order did exist would present itself and I could not walk away—just yet. In a dark corner I found a pile of broken clocks: clocks without hands, hands without dials, and silvered faces twisted. I extracted intact crystals, curling springs, and a baroque iron casing embossed with doves. Crouched over the gears, grease, and mud, I was trapped in a maelstrom of Latin cliches: *tempus fugit, vita brevis, lacrimae rerum*.[3, 4] I examined each crumpled face, random numbers and dials etched into dust. Most things give up the ghost and disappear, but these clocks, stopped at 4:23 or 11:06 or 2:39, were the ghosts. What did I expect to see in their altered faces? The backside of the moon? The foiled face of Father Time?

Although skates and skillets hung in optimistic bunches above my head and the broken clocks had been dumped in one place only, there were few pockets of order and the path through them consisted of fractured planes of mirrors, planks of wood and books shiny as obsidian, wet as blood.

Beyond the clocks, I came across the pile of swollen 78 rpm records from the early 1900s. I had already brought home one of these discs with inky edges and my husband put it on the turntable. To our delight, a sweet, rather forlorn dance came through undistorted, although very thin. At first it sounded like the kind of tune played by a homesick memsahib on a hand-cranked Victrola in a hill station west of Madras. But then, as we listened, we realized that it sounded more like live music broadcast a few seconds ago from very far away, as a New Year's Eve broadcast from the ballroom in London might have sounded to the soldiers in the trenches in France in 1918—if such a broadcast had been possible.

Early phonograph records are composed of layers of fiberboard soaked in shellac. Shellac is made from the pulverized bodies of the tiny female scale insect *Tachardiae lacca*, from India. I peeled the records apart. They came apart like layers of slate. Between two sheets a miniature red spider made a speedy escape. I saw another and then another spider, neon specks tinseling over the black grooves. Just as in shale and slate one finds trace fossils of footprints and trails, these grooves in the records were fossilized sound waves. This collection was part of the paleontology of sound. Records, though, are more ephemeral than slate; if left in a moist environment eventually even the grooves dissolve.

Systems of classification are inventions. Many people, beginning with the seventeenth-century philosopher Francis Bacon (who referred to certain cabinet collections as "sites of broken knowledge"), would despise this barn.[5] Whatever rational order does occur, occurs at random. Although like a hacked-up encyclopedia, which *might* contain everything in the whole world, the contents of this barn are neither organized nor, for the most part, redeemable. But I do believe the twentieth-century painter Francis Bacon, he of the fabulous trashy studio, would have loved this place—for the very qualities that would have drawn scorn from the earlier Bacon. However fragmented, vestiges from two hundred years of history are all in here: brought in by ship, mined from the ground, and all dragged in by Buckminster: a compendium of broken knowledge from New England, Great Britain, France, Spain, and Cuba.[6]

In his early years as an antiques dealer, Buckminster collected and then, to reclaim storage space, deaccessioned a ton of rags. The residue from this enterprise remains glued together in sticky bunches to the floor. I have a profound aversion to sodden fabrics—especially to these: shirts, flags, and bedspreads shiny with rain or soaked in earth, disgorging wadding in dank clots, their folds ripe with spores and streaked with yellow ooze like pus. But sometimes when I found a satin-lined purse or a piece of silken quilt, I remembered the late Edward Purcell's idea about silkworms and lost languages. Purcell, the physicist and my father-in-law, speculated that the vibrations of the voices of the human workers in the silk industry of a thousand years ago might be preserved in the threads that passed through the silkworms' spinnerets. Perhaps, like a wax cylinder from an early recording machine, the threads picked up and preserved archival traces of untranscribed and now vanished dialects. (The average speed at which the worms produce a strand of silk is measured at 6mm to 20mm per second.) Now, a modern scientist might be able to analyze these measurable frequencies and play back a piece of an ancient silk as one might play a phonograph record. Edward liked to refer to his hypothesis as "the riddle of the sphincters."

There is no extinct language to be gleaned from playing back a piece of moldy silk on a record player, of course, but Edward's hypothesis of how to recover lost words allowed me to ignore its repellent qualities long enough to stretch the machine-stitched sample taut and examine the threads for infinitesimal signs of wobble.

In June of 1995, Buckminster and I walked behind the barn where his rhubarb grows to Jack's beanstalk proportions. The weed- and junk-filled depression was the original site of a henhouse, a pigpen, and stalls for horses and cows. The lower beams on this side of the barn exhibited splintered evidence of generations of cattle rubbing and urinating against the wood. Every season the shaved piss-planks wear thinner, and the barn becomes more swaybacked. We moved to the west wall to examine the crowbars Buckminster was using to lift and adjust the huge granite boulders that support the edges of the building and that lie directly on the topsoil. These boulders, he said, shift with the seasons. To maintain proper alignment of the walls, he said of the previous owner, his uncle by marriage, "the old man would jack up the rocks a little bit more." He expresses no confidence in the habits of his predecessor. "Have you ever seen a barn that has collapsed?" he asked more than once. "It's very sad to see a wall lying flat on the ground still hung with tools." Once he added with sorrow, "It's shocking—really."

We have never discussed entropy, that inevitable force of energetic change, but as he described his strategy for straightening the barn, which involved using levels, winches, and rope—as if raising a fallen behemoth—he ended his description not with a pantomime flourish of ropes and winches but with a shrug. As of the summer of 2001, no renovation has taken place, unless—and I don't know—all reconstruction *must* begin with excavation, for Buckminster has removed whopping thicknesses of rotten sills. I photographed the foundation each time I visited, because it was never the same. As the contours of the building shifted, the wall boards widen until gaping, and traps, scythes, and clocks fell out. Finally I could read brand names, warnings, titles, instructions, and newspaper before going inside. Inside I found newspapers from World War One and a water-damaged book of aerial views of French battlefields. I found boxes of unexposed glass photographic plates showing violet

mist and a partially used makeup kit of undertakers' waxes—
"Now that's weird," Buckminster said. It *was* weird—I hadn't
heard him use that word before. We came upon a wooden crate
containing ochre—soft lumps of crimson dye—another kind of
makeup used by the Red Paint people, thousands of years ago,
found near Mount Katahdin. We found a large white stone,
too: "Magnesium," he said. "It will turn purple in the sun."

He seemed discouraged. I tried to comfort him by saying
that his place reflects both the world and the museum;[7] I tell
him that no one person could care for all this. Even museum
curators can't care for all of their things.[8]

If the frame of the barn is like the armature of a large
museum mount, the inside is also like the organic remains of
a colossal creature, with the first floor oozing, the second moist
and hairy, and the third like the cavity of a porous skull. On the
second floor of the barn on a recent visit, I examined the hairy
things: horsehair, straw and twigs from disemboweled furniture made into nests on rafters, a bearskin rug with spikes of
glossy black fur, and a barrel of thick blond plaited tresses, like
the hair of two dozen maidens from the Black Forest—a cache
that turned out to be hanks of hemp for making rope.

Strings of blended mold and plaster draped themselves across
sofas, trunks, and picture frames. I found enormous hunks of tal-
low candles with misshapen sides, soft and visceral. Under the
eaves on the south side against a cracked wall like information
tucked inside a museum mount was a ruined collection of books.

This wall and the attic of the antiques shop harbor many
books, representing two distinct kinds of libraries, intermingled.
The first is of books one might almost still read, and most of

these I have found at the shop: *He Went with Marco Polo* (written by my great-aunt, Louise Andrews Kent), *The Bridge of San Luis Rey* (which I'd read in eighth grade), *They Were Expendable*, and *The Gay Bandit*. I remembered the flavors, if not the details, of the first two stories; I could settle into their cadences in the same way a carrier pigeon, returning home, recognizes the contents of its cage. Like the pigeon, I won't stay long. These days, I do not want to spend too much time with fiction; I already know too well how to speculate about things that did not happen and about people I have never met.[9]

I browsed as I used to do at the public library, aged eleven and twelve, looking for Captain Horatio Hornblower, dashing sailor, dark rake. *The Gay Bandit* was not a Hornblower book. I don't know what kind of book it was; it was bent over double with a gaudy cover of a cowboy, hands cupped around his gun. I found romances from the thirties and forties. Pre–*Peyton Place* and *Blackboard Jungle*, there's nothing to them. They are prim sagas of delayed sexual gratification—resolved, one hopes, sometime after the last line of the last chapter. As I retrieved these damaged books, I felt cozy to the verge of claustrophobia.

Under the eaves, on the west side of the barn, I lifted a dozen volumes as a single unit from the top shelf of a crumbling bookcase. Pages swollen, covers glued together, these books sagged into a single segmented organism of conjoined parts, a sow bug bundle, *a books*. Covered with films of mouse and spider leavings they resisted as, choking, I wrenched them from their base. The books had been in the barn since the early 1950s, Buckminster says, imprinted, I then estimated, by the passage of at least two hundred changes of season.

Six books sharing a flat mud bottom were compressed into an S-shaped curve and the inmost book rested on the lap of its neighbor. The partial titles had, by coincidence, a mystical ring; one read *Moon*...another, *Shrine*. The only legible title was *Black Is White*. I would have had to crack them open to see what had been eaten, who was within, or what they'd left behind. When I tear into the heart of a separated book, whatever does not pulverize survives in shallow alcoves of text. The partial phrases read as cryptic haiku.

The floor beside the compressed bookshelves is pitted and dark; disintegrated boards have fallen through to the first floor and wind has pushed the wall out into thin air. The barn, as it folds in on itself, seems like a living thing to be both growing and shrinking and, always, shifting weight. When, on the second floor, I whacked my head against the low cross beam and had to sit down for a while, Buckminster assured me that it happens to him "all the time."

There must be some evidence of narrative inside these books. I get to work. The pages are delicate, sealed in clumps, with the hollows between webbed with chitinous shrouds. There is no way to penetrate the pages without destroying them. Inside is a story of organic processes unintended by any author. I peer into these transitional hollows where the elements have been traded—type for ash—and wherever such a translation occurs I search for some visible resolution of decay.[10] I am examining this fulcrum of decrepitude as if it were a *thing*. Inside these small-scale caves I observe a process of dissolution that is going on, all the time, in the cosmos everywhere—from words to worms to stars.

On the third floor (planks merely placed over beams and reachable only by a ladder set upright over a gaping hole), I found a suitcase of things so unkeepable I knew that I would keep them—pentimentoed shreddings of paper, cloth, and rubber. The case was stuffed with gnawed mouse nests, soaked and dried cardboards, a dissolving rubber enema bag, knitted hat scraps coated in blued paper and also chewed—an index of elements useful for fine-stuffing the head of a large scarecrow. The latches on the suitcase worked. That's good. Nothing would fall out as I descended the ladder.

The sweepings of memory are like these trashy bits—random shreds of light and dark, bright and broken things. Buckminster's near-smothering by the pig, my fear of the boy with the missing fingers haunt us to this day. When we were children the memory box was loosely packed and there was room to accommodate the flavors of any scene. As adults we think we know more but have stopped perceiving unconditionally. I remember the back and front of the boy's head, the tilted sidewalk and the weeds behind the tree. As an adult I have that two-degree angle of sharpness and each memory is more like a shard than a panorama. Even so, like this suitcase, my memory bank is full.[11]

So now it's up to Buckminster to roll the foundation boulders back and forth until he thinks they're stable for another season. In 1997 he took what seemed like drastic measures to stabilize the barn by placing several beams under the outside edge of the south-facing wall. Inside the building, beside the weakened sill, he dug a hole, five feet deep and twelve feet wide. A mountain of displaced detritus rose up on the far side near the center of the barn floor, freshly stacked. Around the cavernous hole the piles were folded over again. I thought he'd done this work in order to approach the shifting boulders underneath from two sides at once. No, no, he said, he dug the hole to retrieve a few things that had slipped down between the outside wall and the floor. By the winter of 1998 he had placed a steel beam upright on the brink of his excavations. This beam, braced on the granite ledge at one end, remained suspended in space at the top, a few feet short of the rafter it was designed to support. Buckminster claimed it would not fall, but it swayed when I grasped it like a boatman's pole in stiff mud. I watched the rain dripping in a steady stream above this spot, down through three floors to the ground, splattering around the beam and into the hole. The dirt from the ground turned tannish red inside the hole, powdered and packed like the termite leavings in the French history of economics book, the floor above piled with islands.

By 1999 the floor had been partially cleared, scraped down so that the dust, like fur, smelled of the fundamental perspiration of all things with the occasional hint of the long-gone livestock. Buckminster had begun to repair the barn, and, as I looked at the floor, I saw we were going down to the skin of it. Most of my finds have been eviscerated by animals, all things gnawed and some to the bone, the nub, the last straw. A few are as bald as if worked over by parasites burrowing into the cracks between muscle and tendon. And still, on the blade of an old ice skate was a film of dirt, the tool box I opened was full of powdered rust, the wet book covered with beads of mud. You can always count on the dirt.

In the seventeenth century, John Evelyn, enthusiastic expert and lover of earth and trees, described every dirt of England: smelling sweet with earth mold, or foul if tainted by sulfur, with metals and decomposing peat, marl, holy mud, common soil, and that all-time incubator, from which Adam sprung, good old *primal ooze*. Evelyn, the author of *Terra: A Philosophical Discourse of Earth*, is a joyous writer. I had never thought of dirt as much of a subject until I read Evelyn's celebration of all variations of the "rich ooze the fatt'ning valley fills ... good and excellent earth." Owls Head is a smaller place than all of England, but there are many soils at Buckminster's, field dirt, sand, chalk, gravel, ash, pulverized shell, brick, ore, aluminum powder, lead, all the oxides of all the metals, sulphate, carbonate, sand, and the dust that contains the essence of dissolution here.

By the fall of 2001, Buckminster was digging everywhere.[12] He had excavated the threshold inside the entryway to his own house so that the front outer door opened inward onto a hole at least four feet deep and just as wide. It seemed he was in the process of digging a moat between the outer and inner walls, for, bridged by two planks over the abyss, he had created a new obstacle course between the dooryard and kitchen. To cross over, he walked the planks, and then, ever courteous, insisted that I wait until, with a Sir Walter Raleigh–like flourish, he placed a small piece of plywood across the abyss so that I didn't fall in.

We went back into the barn, which on that autumn day felt like a drafty tent. Daylight poured in where pieces of the walls had fallen away. The staircase to the second floor was free-standing now, with no step at the bottom or the top. The elements of the building stood around me like pieces of a set.

"Under the Big Top only two days count, today and tomorrow."[13, 14] Excavation of the sills had advanced. Buckminster had wanted to use logs hewn from his two thirty-foot-tall hemlocks chopped down (without permission) by his neighbor last winter, "just because he thought the tops would make attractive Christmas trees." The wood looked straight enough when growing, Buckminster said, but once felled, it was too crooked to function as sills. A second and all-new excavation inside the barn further divided the floor into smaller reapportioned islands of matter. Wherever the floor had weakened most, Buckminster had removed the boards. On the second floor, he patted the low cross beam. In spite of its pernicious placement as a breaker of heads, the beam, to my untrained eye, appeared to be vital to the stability of the building. "This," he said, "does nothing. I'm thinking of taking it out."

Back downstairs the earth in the original basement hole and on the floor above is stained deep rose as lumps of ochre had been dragged across the boards and into the hole, perhaps, like the charcoal in the captain's house, on the footpads of raccoons. Last night's rain has brought out green and black hues in the boulders down in the hole and it is radiating color. More things have fallen into the hole and, at the peak of Indian summer, hardy vines coil around them reaching for the light. An owl upstairs on a windowsill, as in an EX LIBRIS emblem, would complete the scene, but owls come by less frequently than mourning doves. As it is, few doves remain—heard diffuse and at a distance, settling on the barn at night, gone again at dawn.

NOTES

I. BREAKING GROUND

I.

Termite-eaten book.

2. In the first book of the series by Martha Finley, Elsie, a
   beautiful motherless girl and devout Christian, is forced by
   her tyrannical father (often absent, a nonbeliever and very

handsome) to play the piano on the Sabbath. When she refuses to play, he commands her to sit at the keyboard until she obeys. She falls asleep, falls off the bench, strikes her head, and sustains brain fever, after which her father, stricken by remorse, begins to love his comatose daughter with a somewhat weird fervor. The first volume ends with Elsie, healthy again, crying herself to sleep because her father forgot to say good night. He kisses her lovingly in the last line but she, now sleeping, will never know. Now, I ask you, why stop at the corners? Who would not want to eat the entire book?

3. Termites do not turn into butterflies, of course, but some butterflies do come from unpromising pellets—not unlike the rolls of half-digested paper that stuck to the dark corners of the hollowed-out book.

4. Here, Johanna Branson, the author of the unpublished essay "The Fetishes of History" was using the term *fetishism* in a postmodernist art historical sense, one that depends on a working knowledge of texts by Marx and Freud. Marx's thesis describes the ways in which commercial commodities have become iconic objects for capitalist societies and Freud the ways in which objects become symbolic substitutes for sexual obsession.

5. Krzysztof Pomian, *Collectors and Curiosities: Paris and Venice, 1500–1800* (Cambridge: Polity Press, 1991).

2. INFILTRATION

I.

Postcard view of the Owls Head Light.

Owls Head postmistress, Mrs. Ann Farr, in front of what is now Buckminster's house (photographer unknown).

2. To make my argument seem more persuasive I expounded on the difference between a domestic souvenir and a signifying object (see Pomian, *Collectors and Curiosities*).

3. Buckminster told a journalist that he began amassing stuff in 1950—"Let's say fifty-one according to my tax forms." I have always addressed him as Mr. Buckminster when I am with him, and as Buckminster on paper.

4. Aunt Daisy's brass bed would not constitute part of Buckminster's "inventory" because he threw it out the window before he went into business. He has included it anyway, "to take up some of the slack between my inventory and what I had lost."

5. Ten years later he did take the storm window apart. As I suspected, I had wanted his compliance—not the stencil. I bought it anyway and eventually gave it to friends who collect memorabilia of Maine.

6.

Window with vines growing inside and out.

7.

View through window into the captain's house.

8. In the museum, animal scat is acceptable as an artifact only if fossilized, bottled, or as an integral part of the specimen. Experts analyze coproliths (fossilized scat of dinosaurs), owl pellets, and the insect waste embedded in termite- and worm-eaten texts to reveal both the manner of digestion and the patterns of foraging. If fresh pellets—of a raccoon, perhaps—appeared on the floor in a museum, the curator would be as scandalized as if deposited by one of us. In the museum, except for the occasional pet salamander, lungfish, parrot, or ant farm (all confined), nothing organic and breathing, except for humans, may stalk the well-proofed halls.

9. From the excellent article by Larry Ouellette, *Coastal Bureau*, 27 June 1981, in which he refers to Buckminster as "a virtual connoisseur of culch."

10.

Lead plumbing, scaffolding against antiques shop.

11. Flann O'Brien, *The Dalkey Archive* (Great Britain: MacGibbon and Kee, 1964).

12.

Oil tanks in back of Buckminster's house.

13.

Buckminster standing in his copper pile.

3. DISINTEGRATION

I.

Book-nest.

2.

Typewriter.

3.

White horse before it lost its legs.

4. A hundred years ago, I might have used a *Claude* glass, a mirror made of black obsidian invented by the eighteenth-century painter Claude Lorraine. This device reduces the colors of the sky, fields, and trees into levels of luminosity more easily interpreted and transcribed on paper. Today a #90 viewing filter achieves the same effect.

5.

Buckminster's hands on rubber stripped from wire.

6.

Window for Billy *construction/photograph, circa 1984.*

7. Here and there appears a wheel without the car, a free-standing black bathing suit, a railing without a staircase, a child on the lap of a woman who has no face, three lounging boys, arms and legs washed pencil-thin. The photos in sequence, like a stuttering narrative, preserve details at random: arms, hats, wheels and railings, the dark road beyond several human shadows, and above these the full-leafed tops of trees. Foliage, ephemeral in reality, lasts longer as saturated silver.

4. DIGGING DEEPER

1. "One of the most interesting things in this locality is the prehistoric shell heaps about half a mile up the river from the town [of Damariscotta]... The top layer was deposited by the Abenakis; within history, but nobody knows who is responsible for the bottom layers or how old they are. Inspecting these mounds is almost like seeing a blueprint of pre-European culture—a blueprint that you can almost, but not quite, read and fully interpret" (Louise Dickinson Rich, *The Coast of Maine: An Informal History and Guide* [reprint, New York: HarperCollins, 1993], 247).

2. In medieval times mules were said to live forever. In *Vernon, Florida*, the 1981 documentary film by Errol Morris, Joe Payne, an ancient fisherman, hauled a dead mule out of a pond. According to Mr. Payne, the mule was "tough as a bear... one hundred and fourteen walleye perch in him... I could hear them flutterin' in there." The poet Seamus

Heaney described the skeleton of the extinct great Irish deer pulled from a peat bog as "an astounding crate full of air" (Seamus Heaney, "Bogland," in *Opened Ground: Selected Poems, 1966–1996* [New York: Farrar, Straus & Giroux, 1998]).

3.

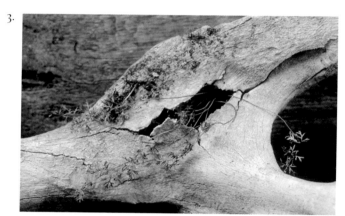

Bone from horse or cow with small plant.

4. Certain slabs are as biblical texts from a landlocked sea. On one of these, I find an ancient-seeming fragment—"carefully planned eons…"—that reads as advice from God to the survivors of the earth purged of the wicked by Noah's flood.

5.

Comic strip embedded in slab.

6. He was referring to the reclusive Collyer brothers from the Bronx who collected mountains of papers and died in the early 1940s when one brother, a cripple, starved because the other became trapped under an avalanche of newspapers and magazines.

7.

Buckminster's sales book.

8. Dolls, intended as props to teach maternal ways to little girls, make no practical sense in this place. Where animals, insects, and plants multiply and thrive, humans do not. One person now lives where once there were three families.

9. Why *don't* dolls have bones?

10. Buckminster did say she never married.

II.

Doll with dew in hair and lace.

5. TRANSGRESSION

I. "This is a storehouse, not a dwelling," said a friend, when during an ice storm we were invited into the warmth of Buckminster's kitchen. It does smell like an old museum storage space. One cannot make out the contents of the three rooms on the ground floor without turning on a light. A lamp with an unshaded bulb set beside the telephone rests against a wall of magazines and papers, and several times I have heard a chirping like the dying battery of a smoke alarm. Buckminster has a smoke alarm, but what I have heard, he said, were crickets, one of which lived in the stairwell for several years.

2. As a girl my friend Valerie lived on Burnt Island, not far from Owls Head. Val had bought everything for her first apartment from Helen and spoke of her kind nature. She didn't know Buckminster as well; he kept his distance, out on the piles of metal in his workshop or on the road—he was always "off." Helen was the practical partner, Val said, the energy behind inventory, tags, sales slips, and receipts, the jolly soul of the shop, which may be why now the order in that building feels most violated.

According to Buckminster, Helen's kindness was not always reciprocated by the world at large. "She didn't put up with any bullshit," Buckminster says, and I get the feeling that this was his choice of phrase—from the scrap metal side of the business. An early tenant of the small cottage stole many antiques one summer, another reduced Helen to tears by relentless visits and aggressive bargaining. "The kind of person—if you *gave* it to them, they'd ask *you* to pay *them* to take it away." Helen loved cats; she also loved children. "But," he said, "it didn't go that way."

3.

Buckminster's front door with wreath.

4. My paraphrase of John le Carré, *The Secret Pilgrim* (New York: Knopf, 1991), 175.

6. UNDERGROUND

1.

Buckminster in doorway of captain's house.

2.

Detached trophy figures.

3. Buckminster later told me that he had bought the entire lot from a factory when it went out of business. The metal was almost entirely silver-plated pewter.

4. The lighthouse was built in 1826 during the John Quincy Adams administration.

5. Richard Meryman, author of *Andrew Wyeth: A Secret Life* (New York: HarperCollins, 1996). The Wyeth family legacy is enshrined in Rockland (Farnsworth Museum), at Chadds Ford (Brandywine Museum), and at the Olsen House, site of Wyeth's famous painting *Christina's World.* Meryman's book includes wonderful descriptions of the endless power struggle that takes place between the art world (museums and critics) and the artist.

6. Johnson quote from a documentary film on Buckminster Fuller. *Thinking Out Loud*, American Masters 1996, dir. Kirk Simon and Karen Goodman.

7. I learned early on that bogeymen were real—and infiltrated the most genteel neighborhoods. More than once, when I was walking to elementary school past the Radcliffe College buildings, a janitor would charge up from a cellar room, stop, as if chained, on the top step and lifting his arms as though under a shroud, he would silently roar.

8. Silvio Bedini, *Early American Scientific Instruments and Their Makers* (Washington, D.C.: Smithsonian Institution, 1964).

9.

Chandler Farr and Ann Farr (circa 1910), photographer unidentified.

10. As I am "getting the goods" on Buckminster, gathering together as many elements of hearsay and direct observation

as possible and then laying down the pieces one at a time, as in a game of solitaire, many cards are still missing. As a biographer it seems I am always playing with a flawed deck.

7 . PASSING THROUGH

I.

Shadow figure in the swamp.

2. A stump fence naturally forms from the zigzag trunks of trees cleared to allow the meadow to grow.

3.

Dinghy in weeds.

4. I would be less impatient with the chrysalises if there had been more to see. I do not have that kind of X-ray faith that can dissolve the opacity of things nor do I have the experience to know whether these would hatch.

5. The famous naturalist Hans Sloan, who inherited Petiver's collection in the early 1700s, described the disheveled condition of the specimens thus: "Mr Petiver put them in heaps, with sometimes small labels of paper, where there were many of them injured by Dust, Insects, Rain, etc."

6. In the first catalogue of the Royal Society (1681), Nehemiah Grew described the wings of a beetle known to him as the Great West Indian Goat-chafer as "square-knobbed...[with] ...fine hair like the pile of velvet," the rough places on its carapace "cast with a great number of small black knobs like

the Mourning pin-heads." Grew writes of beetles as mechanical wind-ups, referring to the Tingle-worme as the "Oil Clock" because its eyes drip an oily fluid, while the color of this *Scaraboeus melanocyaneus* is "exactly like that color which watchmakers and others give to their steel-works."

8. STILL POINT

1. Perhaps human history is like a red pig outfitted with organic and mechanical parts, a pig barreling along like a full-stoked engine; an amalgam of braying gongs and generations of teeming and dying cells.

2. The young Russian men in the termite-eaten book from the MCZ left their father's farms at the beginning of the industrial revolution, thereby breaking the continuity of their inheritance.

3.

Windows against window.

4. *Nympho-bar-maid.* I was somewhat startled by this revelation. Sounded peculiar coming from this high-minded guru of the pool hall. Later I realized that this was the phonetic pronunciation of an actual drug.

5.

Interior of barn #1.

6. Quote from "Burnt Norton," in T. S. Eliot, *Four Quartets* (New York: Harcourt, Brace, 1943).

Buckminster, who plays in two tournaments a week, wins almost every time, usually forty to sixty dollars.

9. THE FOUNDRY

1. When I asked him what he meant by "the Holy Grail," he said oh, he was just joking; "after all, Sir Walter Raleigh never did find it, did he?"

2. He has done the historical research but when he says it is the earliest existing brass foundry in the United States and probably also in all of Europe, he is quoting an expert from the Smithsonian who came by several decades ago. He did not invite Bedini to see the foundry, as he did not want, he said, to "spoil the occasion." I worried that he had lost a good opportunity to promote his cause.

3.

Unopened packets of nails/hooks made by Webb.

4.

View inside and outside room where Webb's legacy is kept. Photograph of General Neil Dow in corner.

5. In the closet, I found boxes of early-nineteenth-century invoices and letters, ahistorically lumped together and sequentially stained by rain or the urine of small animals. Most of the papers—from shopping lists of a Maine housewife in the 1950s to Civil War letters, including one from the battlefield at Bull Run in Virginia in which the death of a general, Hiram Berry from Rockland, Maine, is movingly described—were excavated by Buckminster and placed elsewhere years ago. A heavy drill press now blocks the door. Whatever's left inside has been reentombed for posterity.

6. Variously referred to as *Major bragaduce*, *Magabagaduce*, and *Majabigwaduce* in eyewitness accounts.

7. According to the *Columbia Encyclopedia* Revere, a staunch opponent of the British, also studied and practiced such diverse talents as engraving and dentistry, ending his profitable days as the owner of a brass and copper foundry in Canton, Massachusetts.

8.

Systematic arrangement of Webb's tools with examples of his wares.

9. In the *Farmer's Almanac* forecast of weather was made by studying sunspots.

10. His claim unsubstantiated at present.

11. "A flight of pidgeons that to my thinking had neither beginning nor ending, length nor breadth, and so thick I could see no sun," wrote John Josselyn in 1675. The account of the flight of the pigeons in 1817 is described, too, by John James Audubon in his *Birds of America* (completed in 1838), and by bird artist Alexander Wilson. See also Henry Stommel and Elizabeth Stommel, *Volcano Weather: The Story of the Year Without a Summer, 1816* (Newport, RI: Seven Seas Press, 1983).

10. RAG AND BONE SHOP

1. *Precious Moments*, I've since discovered, refers to limited editions of sentimental figurines known in the trade as "collectible smalls."

2. It is moments like this when I think I know how it must be for Buckminster. I feel that my clock has been set more closely to his; any object selected from the stack gives him almost too much to consider, just as, in the studio, I spend a lot of time gazing in a peaceful stupor, taking time out from the world of action…impotent before the world of things.

3.

Miniature museum by R. Purcell (approximately 3 feet long by 2 feet high).

4.

Studio wall (approximately 11 feet long by 7 feet high).

5.

Bookcase containing few legible volumes.

6. In any good natural history museum, the label on the door
    would say *NYCTEA SCANDIACA*, and the snowy owl, as
    promised, would lie behind that door. The cigar box marked
    5¢ Pippins contains neither cigars nor apples. *Boite Nature*
    does not contain much of any "nature" but a distillation
    from Buckminster's dooryard: fish-line reels, threaded nuts,
    minute oil cans, rim of tea strainer, scroll-sawn wood, bottle
    caps flat as coins, and in an interior box pieces of oxidized
    skins of paint, stored by size.

7. green melted slab–mostly
        copper–of plumbing
        pipes, glass, and stones
    two steel airplanes–auto
        hood ornaments
    rubber horse
    half a plaster boy scout
        with battered face
    half-scissors
    broken thread on a spool
    fancy paper suitcase
    doctor's satchel
    eight warped fishing
        knives in a warped
        wooden case
    chair stacked with worm-
        tracked shingles
    trawling net attached to
        cement block

    ivory slats from a fan
    strings from a piano
    dried ray like a monkey
    stone with a stain like
        profile of sleeping
        monkey
    copper scales balanced on
        iron base
    ten fire extinguishers
    linked chain and
        ladder from a fishing
        boat
    half-dissolved plaster
        lobster
    door to iron stove
        *Keep ashpit free from
        ashes*
    three highway warning
        flasher lights

wooden keg holding:

    metal name post from cemetery

    wire lamp cage

    ax with split wooden handle

    thin ax heads

double-coned telephone receiver on rusted cord

telephone box (belongs to above receiver)

head of a broom like army brush haircut

hoops of barbed wire

dark scythe

frail wheel–bicycle

shears held together by rope

ring and bit from horse's harness

harness with copper studs (now blue)

fire-gnarled license plates

half-moon hubcaps from VWs and Chevrolets

pottery bowl with broken base, scallop shells covered with inch-wide barnacles

wooden shoe-last

hat forms (two)

iron stove corners (two)

crumpled tin lanterns (two)

shells from second World War shaped into vases

Hansel and Gretel with Witch weather house (Austrian Alps motif)

croquet balls (twelve, battered, no stripes)

copper toilet-bowl floats (twenty-four, some with intact stems)

copper ladle (green)

keys (varying degrees of rust)

file with rougherings like fish scales

dasher from a wooden butter churn

sides of churn

birdhouses (six)

watering cans (three, no bottoms)

apple tree (segments three foot and six foot lengths)

antlers

smaller antlers with
skullcap of animal

wooden mallet with
detachable handle

wooden mallet held
together by chains

wooden frame for test
tubes

brick fragments, red and
yellow

brick with elongated
worm mark

brick with cat footprints

flower of stamped metal
on an electrical stem

wine bottle (melted,
swollen into
astigmatism)

rat traps (two, moldy)

watch with obliterated
ceramic face

shotgun shell casings

wooden boat (base and hull
carved from one piece)

broken gas gauge (like
the head and shoulders
of a robot and filled
with string)

wooden clockworks
(three sets)

wooden blueberry
winnower (6 feet × 4
feet × 2 feet with drum)

tricycle (front wheel and
shaft)

wooden newel post

wooden post (square-
topped, plain)

copper and wooden
icebox door

glass test tubes nested in
octagonal cardboards
like honeycomb

aluminum chimney pipes

tin stove pipes

twelve copper water-
closet boxes

a skin-feather flap with
armature of twine and
cotton, once a songbird

bottles painted with thin
blue glaze

celluloid baby with diaper

celluloid bears with
rolling eyes

split plaster hippo

ditto tiger

headless camels
two hollow copper
    wedges (five feet high)
zinc boat float
zinc rake head patched
    with window
    screening
rusted thermometer
    with mercury—today,
    fifty degrees
    Fahrenheit
leather bag crimped shut
    from turn-of-the-
    century plumber
Shaker blue–painted
    sawhorse held
    together by rope
limp table with crippled
    legs
pewter bowl with mussel
    shells
bentwood nail-studded
    chair, missing seat,
    one front leg raised off
    floor

ten defunct flashlights
    (two with cowboy
    themes)
airplane goggles (for
    open-cockpit flight
    with screens on side to
    keep out wind)
tangled pile of trophy
    figures: bowlers,
    baseball, and golf
green-tinted basketball
    trophy against gold
    metal disk
printing plate of a
    monkey breaking a
    tree limb
celluloid lamp-clock of
    Uncle Sam holding
    flag
copper Indian labeled
    "Wah-Jack" holding
    bent tool

8. This wood came from a canyon fire above Malibu.

9. As it came from Arizona, a place where it almost never rains, this is mysterious.

10. The bread was given to a Harvard minister by a political prisoner in France, in 1918, and to me by the minister's widow, in 1970.

11.

Cheetah on shelf.

12. If, for example, the eye orbit of the fossil horse looks like a volcanic depression, doesn't this mean appearance has delivered two realities for the price of one? If the physical evidence is in front of the camera and the content, as recorded by the camera, unmanipulated, how can this approach possibly be called "less factual" than one that includes a jackknife to mark the scale? It is photography itself that is "less factual."

The application of metaphor, from art, from history, even the fiction of natural history, was rarely effective in my battle with certain curators. But, as I had discovered, and Stephen Gould knew too, because many things look like other things, the archive from a single museum, even the contents of a single drawer, may expand when photographed to reveal an infinite number of things.

13.

Stick shaped like Hindu dancer with roots and electrical wire.

14.

Tin can I refused to sell for $300.

15. Months later when I had given up ever finding the flash-light a package arrived from *The Atlantic* magazine containing my own (unopened) proposal for an article about ruined objects as well as the flashlight, which I had enclosed because I wanted the editor to take the project seriously.

II. IN THE TRENCHES

1. The photographs, taken by British reconnaissance planes, show the hatched edges of fortifications, depressions of the trenches, and the pitted fields blasted by bombs. Covered with mold and faded throughout, I have used them as backgrounds in the war/object collages.

2. Paul Fussell, *The Great War and Modern Memory* (New York: Oxford University Press, 1975).

3.

Watch without hands on rotogravure of French village liberated from Germans, 1945.

4. Museum primates have always been among my favorite photographic subjects. They contributed to the larger photographs because monkeys and apes whose eyes were stuffed with cotton resembled WW I soldiers in gas masks, confirming our close connections.

5. "...fix what has been broken": my paraphrase of Laurie Anderson's ("The Dream Before," 1989) paraphrasing of Walter Benjamin, from his essay "Theses on Philosophy of History #9" (1940), in *Illuminations, Essays and Reflections* edited by Hannah Arendt and translated by Harry Zohn, New York: Schocken, 1968.

6.

Detail from Enola Gay *collage on reverse glass painting, circa 1984.*

7.

Eve, *temporary collage for large-format photograph. Glass, wood, metal, paper, and cloth, circa 1984.*

8.

Malmaison 1, *collage in leaded window.*   *Detail of ape hanging in archway.*

12. A WONDERFUL LIFE

1. Inside, members of entire dynastic groups of pigeons as well as more than 330,000 other birds rest in (fitful) archival peace.

13. TRANSCRIPTION

1. In our conversation I catch certain rhythms of intention, truncated yet momentous as a cross section taken from the past twenty years of my collecting, fifty years of his collecting, and the last two hundred years of cultural accumulation.

14. THE BARN

1. More than once inside this barn I've thought about Robert Wilson's installation of the hollow elephant, the decrepit Bonapartist watchman, mechanical rats, and opera music.

In a small room at the Boston Museum of Fine Arts Wilson demonstrated just how several layers of history may exist simultaneously in a trashy place. Wilson's inspiration: three buildings that stood (consecutively) on la place de la Bastille in Paris—first (until 1789) a four-hundred-year-old prison, second (until 1846) a three-storied plaster elephant built by Napoleon, which, after it became infested by rats, was torn down, and last the opera house. These layers—of prison, hollow pachyderm, music, and the proliferation of rodents—ratcheted up to melodrama the different chronological levels compressed into a single scene.

2.

Exterior of barn, south side.

3.

Stack of books, boxes under the tarp.

4. *Tempus fugit, vita brevis, lacrimae rerum*: time flies; life is short; these are the tears of things (i.e., human events).

5. Francis Bacon wrote about the dangers of expressing too much wonder toward oddities, anomalies, and monsters. Favoring an overall obligation to understand every part of the natural world, he was opposed to irrational impulses when it came to collecting.

6. Although I found relatively few texts in foreign languages, there were many objects from abroad. Ships from Thomaston and Searsport sailed all over the world and returned with souvenirs.

7.

Interior of barn.

8. A fellow Cantabridgian remembers seeing trash cans full of disembodied monkey/ape parts on the sidewalk outside the Peabody Museum. In another incident of dubious waste-management, the taxidermied bodies of four elephant seals (now highly endangered) were sawed into manageable pieces and discarded due to lack of space.

9. There is a torturous trickiness to real-life events. Good fiction writers profit from making selective omissions (see Janet Malcolm, *The Silent Woman: Sylvia Plath and Ted Hughes* [New York: Knopf, 1994]).

10. *Translation:* as in, to transfer from one place/condition to another.

11. To keep any part of memory at all, I break it down into fewer details—for efficiency's sake. As time passes I will lose track, first of the details, then of the whole.

12. Inside the houses things are turned around. It is as if the captain's house, like a Bucky Fuller Dymaxion house, has swiveled round inside its shell, shifting mounds of impedimenta from east to west so that entrance and egress shift their orientations accordingly. Instead of removing two-by-fours from the back door and hauling our way through three rooms before reaching the stairs, Buckminster pries open the door facing the road and—most unusual—we enter through the front door. The staircase to the second floor is built less than three feet from the entranceway, each riser covered with chewed cork, hunks of plaster, and miscellaneous papers, destined for the large cardboard barrel set on the bottom step, and topped by a basin of debris, which I manage to upend. The landing at the top of the stairs is covered by mounds of dung and well-chewed miscellany. There's no need to sniff the air; I exhale as the pungency seems to come from within. The original wallpaper yields to the lightest tug, peeling away in unrepastable strips. The room is dank with lumps of plaster (fresh fallen) on the laid-out tools.

    I work my way back down and through the ground-floor rooms to assess how the byways have shifted: the first room, once day-lit, is now tenebrous, the inner ring of gleaming

trophies faded to dim slivers glimpsed over new embankments. Raccoons have strewn charcoal across the pine floor,
working it into the grain of the wood as if to paint it black.
The corridors have become ever tighter as, looking over
the tops of dikes, I gaze into crevices where large pieces of
furniture used to be. I do not recognize the rooms now,
reconfigured as they are by so much addition—or subtrac-
tion. The layers have slid from one side to the other, as if
the house has listed in heavy seas. I struggle through the
reconfigured maze toward the original back door. So much
has been piled up against it now, I will never get out.

13. Charlton Heston, in *The Greatest Show on Earth* (1952).

14. *The fabulous chameleon—changes its color to fit the scene—
watch him disappear!* At the circus, my friends and I bought
these hapless living lizards (a few inches in length, equipped
with tiny chains) and pinned them to our clothes. Next day
I wore this trophy to Sunday school. But this particular
lizard had already let me down by not turning navy blue
to match my coat. It remained forever grey. Whatever
chromogenic range it had possessed in its tropical habitat
was wiped away by the chill of Cambridge and the First
Unitarian Church. Somewhere between the opening hymn
and offeratory, the lizard slipped from torpid to moribund,
its forelimbs stiffening at ninety degrees to its body, like a
crucifix. I unclipped it and threw it away. I have not worn
a living creature since.

ACKNOWLEDGMENTS

During the years I visited Buckminster, I had the good fortune
to collaborate on three books about museums and collectors
with the late Stephen Jay Gould. The *sanctum sanctorum* in
most venerable museums is no more than a jumble of miscellany and dust. One day, though, in St. Petersburg, in the pupil of
a glass eye from the cabinet of Peter the Great, I saw the case-
ment of the windows and the hall that the eye and I occupied.
I saw that the eye was drinking in the light and putting the
room on display. Back home, Stephen pointed out what I had
not noticed: the reflected room was bare. I continued to look *at*
and *through* and *back at* the camera's subjects, knowing that in
the end the implications as well as the content would be subject to Gould's inventive, scouring scrutiny. Today, the eye of a
fossil horse looks like a dormant volcano to me, and curled strips
of lead from Buckminster's antique plumbing like Gould's favorite snails, called *Cerion*, uncoiling.

How important are the names of things? In a junk shop in
Paris, intrigued by a dim object, I asked to see "that thing." "If
Madame does not know the name," the shopkeeper informed
me, "it can be of no importance to Madame."

I have cajoled many friends and relations to visit Owls Head,
land of unnamable things. If you did visit and you don't read

your name, you probably broke some unspoken rule, or I have forgotten the occasion; I am sorry. I do thank Lynn Martin, Karen Reuter, Desiree Navab, Andrew and John Henry Purcell, Mary Andrews Wolff, Arlene Morris and Steve Stern, Darrel Razdow, Consuelo Isaacson, Ashling Barr, Mary Jo McConnell, Lisa Melandri, Sam Donham, and in spirit Beth Busser Purcell. To Wendy Kaminer, much gratitude for breaking the ice with Buckminster; to Marjory Wunsch for her friendship and participation in this story, and to Val Donham, enthusiastic supporter of the Buckminster legacy, who provided shelter and trekked with me to unfamiliar pool halls. Thanks also to Richard D'Abate and John Mayer from the Maine State Historical Society, Edwin Churchill of the Maine State Museum, Jill Kneerim, Sarah Larsen, Emily Hiestand, and Sabine Hrechdakian, and to Ethan Nosowsky on a busman's holiday. I spent years on a hunch that Owls Head was worth a book. Thanks to all who agreed. Thank you especially to Jennifer Ackerman, whose spirit-lifting counsel helped me weather intrigues of the marketplace. From the beginning Dennis Purcell provided unwavering moral support and infallible practical advice. For two decades now Jim Mairs has encouraged me in almost all my projects. I am proud to sail again under the Quantuck Lane banner. Thanks to editor Brook Wilensky-Lanford and to publicist Janey Tannenbaum. Thanks to Don Kennison for his careful copyediting. Special gratitude to Laura Lindgren, designer, friend, rare find. To my siblings, Katy, Rob, and Jamie Wolff, who know where I am coming from—I hope you like this book. To William Buckminster—I sure hope you like it too.